The
HERITAGE BOOK
2001

The

HERITAGE
BOOK

2001

Edna McCann

HarperCollins*PublishersLtd*

THE HERITAGE BOOK 2001

www.harpercanada.com

HarperCollins books may be purchased
for educational, business, or sales promo-
tional use. For information please write:
Special Markets Department,
HarperCollins Canada,
55 Avenue Road, Suite 2900,
Toronto, Ontario, Canada M5R 3L2.

First edition

"Skating on the Pond" by Gladys Harp is
reprinted by permission of the author.
"February" by Edna Jacques: published
in Canada by Thomas Allen & Son Ltd.
Reprinted by permission.
"Bright October" by Kay Hoffman
is reprinted by permission of the author.
"Footprints" © 1964
by Margaret Fishback Powers.
Published by HarperCollinsPublishersLtd

Canadian Cataloguing in Publication Data

McCann, Edna
The heritage book

Annual.
1977–
Issue for 2000 has title:
The Canadian heritage book.
Published by: HarperCollins, 1999–   .
ISSN 0711-4737
ISBN 0-00-200050-4 (2001 ed.)

1. Devotional calendars—Periodicals.
2. Anecdotes.
3. Maxims, English.
I. Title

PN6331.M32   242'.2   C82-030470-0

99 00 01 02 03 04 WEB 8 7 6 5 4 3 2 1

Printed and bound in Canada
Set in New Caledonia

Introduction

MANY people are looking forward to this year, 2001, as the *real* beginning of the millennium. They reason that, because you don't start counting at zero, this year represents the first year in the new millennium.

This year marks a special anniversary for me as well. This is the twenty-fifth edition of the *Heritage Book*, which is quite astonishing to me. When my husband and family encouraged me to compile my thoughts and those of others who inspired me, I had no idea that people (other than friends and family) might enjoy reading them. I am always surprised and touched when I receive letters from my readers telling me how much they enjoy the book. It's amazing how often I'll read "I feel just the same way about that,"or "My family sounds so much like yours."

It occurred to me that I have many people to thank for my success: my late husband, George, whose love and encouragement gave me the courage to begin writing; my family and friends who provide so many of the stories that I share with you; the many editors whose expertise I depend upon so heavily; the other writers or poets whose thoughts and works add so much; my deepest appreciation to Carole Black for her exquisite illustrations that make this anniversary edition a very special one; and finally, my readers who have made my accomplishment possible.

Thank you all!

January

Monday January 1

AS I awoke this first morning of a wonderful new year, I remembered a "New Year's Prayer" by Lolita Pinney and thought it most appropriate for today.

A whole new year is mine today…
May I be wiser, Lord, I pray!

I'd strengthen friendships old and true,
And learn to cherish new ones, too;
To keep on learning and to grow
A little better as I go.

To cast aside each grudge and grief,
And hold fast to a firm belief
That life is joyous, gracious, good,
When lived in terms of brotherhood!

To welcome fun and play a while,
To lighten work with a happy smile!
To thank the Lord and every day
Remember him and kneel to pray
In gratitude for strength and health
And blessings which are all my wealth.

This year's a gift from God to me
To spend, or use, or set me free...

A whole new year is mine today...
May I be wiser, Lord I pray!

Tuesday January 2

MY daughter Margaret and I spent most of today taking down our Christmas decorations. After the joy and excitement of the Christmas season, I find that this time of putting away our wreaths and wrapping the ornaments to be stored is always tinged with a bit of sadness. Christmas is such a beautiful time of the year that the house seems to look so plain and feel so empty when we have tidied up.

My dear friend Martha gave me some interesting suggestions that she calls her "January Pick-Me-Ups." She too, packs away her Christmas decorations, but she replaces red candles with white ones in her candle holders and leaves many of them on the mantle, side tables and coffee table. As well, she uses one string of the miniature white lights to decorate her Benjamina tree. The lights, along with the tiny white-ribbon bows, give the feeling of a beautiful snow-covered tree, indoors.

"I light a fire in my fireplace everyday, Edna, and I enjoy my tea in my favourite chair where I

can delight in the warmth of the flames. As well, I hang numerous bird feeders close to my windows and the many cardinals, chickadees and blue jays that come to dine on the seeds seem to bring cheer to all of my winter days."

I think I'll try some of Martha's suggestions.

Wednesday January 3

NEVER fear spoiling children by making them too happy. Happiness is the atmosphere in which all good affections grow.

Thomas Bray

Thursday January 4

MY great-grandson Mickey has been looking to buy a used car to drive at university. With the help of his father, he has been scanning the newspapers and auto magazines hoping to find one that is both safe and affordable. A friend in the auto industry has given them some excellent advice on what to look for, and I thought I would pass along a few of his hints to you readers.

Accident records from across the country indicate that you are much less likely to be involved in a crash if you are driving a sedan (four-door car)

The larger the wheelbase of your automobile, the safer you will be. Buy the largest car in the vehicle class that you are considering.

All-wheel drive or front-wheel drive cars are better at keeping you from slipping and sliding.

White or light-coloured cars are easier to see and are less often involved in accidents than dark-coloured cars.

Seat belts and air bags, including side air bags, offer excellent protection.

Of course nothing offers more protection than good, skilled driving.

Friday January 5

LET every dawn of the morning be to you as in the beginning of life. And let every setting of the sun be to you as its close. Then let every one of those short lives leave its sure record of some kindly thing done for others; some good strength or knowledge gained for yourself.

John Ruskin

Saturday January 6

THIS date is the celebration of the Epiphany. In the western church, it is the day to commemorate the coming of the three wise men who were led by the star of Bethlehem to the birthplace of the infant Jesus.

... and, lo, the star, which they saw in the east, went before them, till it came and stood over where the young child was.

When they saw the star, they rejoiced with exceeding great joy.

And when they were come into the house, they saw the young child with Mary his mother, and fell down, and worshipped him: and when they had opened their treasures, they presented him with gifts; gold and frankincense, and myrrh.

Matthew 2: 9-11

Sunday January 7

BUT they that wait upon the Lord shall renew their strength; they shall mount up with wings as eagles; they shall run, and not be weary; and they shall walk, and not faint.

Isaiah 40:31

Monday January 8

THERE is an Arabic parable that says, "Write the bad things that are done to you in sand, but write the good things that happen to you on a piece of marble."

What wise advice. Life gives us all our share of good and bad, but there are times when the challenges we face can seem like mountains. In those times we need to remind ourselves that we have always been given the strength to get us through our difficulties. If we think back on other times when we have triumphed, remembering our joys instead of our sorrows, we may see the good in our life written "on a piece of marble."

Tuesday January 9

NO man can tell whether he is rich or poor by turning to his ledger. It is the heart that makes a man rich. He is rich according to what he is, not according to what he has.

Henry Ward Beecher

Wednesday January 10

MY sister Sarah received a letter from a friend. She has no idea who wrote this funny story but we both enjoyed the "senior humour" enormously. It reads, in part:

"A very weird thing has happened. A strange old lady has moved into my house. I have no idea who she is, where she came from or how she got in. All I know is that one day she wasn't there and the next day she was.

She manages to keep out of sight for the most part, but whenever I pass a mirror, I catch a glimpse of her. And whenever I look in the mirror, there she is obliterating my beautiful face.

I don't want to jump to conclusions, but I think she is stealing money from me. I go to the bank and take out $100.00, and just a few days later, it is all gone. I certainly don't spend money that fast!

For an old lady, she is quite childish. She plays nasty games, like going into my closet and altering my clothes to make them too tight. She also messes up my files and papers so that I can't find anything.

She gets my mail, newspapers and magazines before I do and blurs the print so that I can't read it. She has also done something sinister to the volume on my radio and television. Now all I hear are mumbles and whispers.

She has done other things as well, like make my stairs steeper, my vacuum cleaner heavier and faucets harder to turn. She also applies glue to the lids of all my jars, making them impossible for me to open!

Just when I thought that she couldn't be any meaner, she proved me wrong. She came along when I went to get my driver's license, and just as the shutter clicked, she put her face in front of mine. No one is going to believe that the picture of that old lady is me!"

Thursday January 11

ISAW God write this gorgeous poem this very morning. With the fresh sunbeam for a pencil, on the broad sheet of level snow, the diamond letters were spelled out one by one, 'til the whole was aflame with poetry.

Phillip Brooks

Friday January 12

LOVE is the doorway through which the human soul passes from selfishness to service and from solitude to kinship with all humankind.

Saturday January 13

NEVER look down to test the ground before taking your next step: only he who keeps his eye fixed on the far horizon will find his right road.

Dag Hammarskjöld

Sunday January 14

FOR I am persuaded, that neither death, nor life, nor angels, nor principalities, nor powers, nor things present, nor things to come,

Nor height, nor depth, nor any other creature, shall be able to separate us from the Love of God, which is in Christ Jesus our Lord.

Romans 8:38–39

Monday January 15

TODAY is the birth date of Dr. Martin Luther King, the African-American statesman and Nobel Peace Prize winner. The late Dr. King was the inspirational leader of the civil rights movement and a man of unquestioned character. I think these words of Harry Emerson Fosdick are an appropriate tribute for today.

"There is no more searching test of the human spirit than the way it behaves when fortune is adverse and it has to pass through a prolonged period of disappointments and failures. Then comes the real proof of a man. Achievement, if a man has the ability, is a joy, but to take the hard knocks and come up smiling, to have your mainsail blown away and then rig a sheet on the bowsprit and sail on, this is perhaps the deepest of character."

Tuesday January 16

ON a cold winter evening there was nothing that my husband, George, enjoyed more than meatloaf. This recipe for Potato-Crusted Meatloaf is delicious and looks special enough to serve for company.

2 tbsp. oil, divided in half
1 medium onion, coarsely chopped (about 1/2 cup)
2 cloves minced garlic
1 tbsp. dried oregano
3/4 tsp. salt (optional) divided
1/2 tsp. Pepper divided in half
2 pounds ground beef
2 tbsp. parsley flakes
2/3 cup Italian-seasoned bread crumbs
4 oz. pitted green olives, coarsely chopped
1/2 cup bottled chili sauce
2 eggs
3–4 potatoes (about 2 1/2 pounds), peeled and cut into 2 inch chunks
1 tbsp. milk

Preheat oven to 350°F. In a small frying pan, heat 1 tbsp. oil over medium high heat. Add onion, garlic, oregano, 1/2 tsp. salt, 1/4 tsp. pepper. Cook until onion is golden—about 10 minutes. Remove from heat and set aside.

In a mixing bowl, combine the ground beef, parsley flakes, bread crumbs, olives, chili sauce, eggs, potatoes and milk. Mix in reserved onions. Shape into a loaf, and place in a roasting pan. Bake, basting occasionally with drippings until no longer pink in the center (about 1–1 1/4 hours).

Cook potatoes in boiling salted water until tender (about 20–25 minutes). Drain. Add remaining oil, salt and pepper. Mash until smooth. Remove meatloaf from oven. Using a pastry bag with a large star tip, pipe potatoes over meatloaf or spread over meatloaf with a spatula. Broil until golden (5–7 minutes). Makes 8 servings.

Wednesday January 17

THERE are only two ways to live your life. One is as though nothing is a miracle. The other is as though everything is a miracle.

Albert Einstein

"Winter Morning"

Thursday January 18

NO love, no friendship, can cross the path of our destiny without leaving some mark on it forever.

François Mauriac

Friday January 19

SEVERAL of my senior friends and I have found an extremely pleasant way to spend a cold winter's afternoon. One of the larger book stores in our area has comfortable chairs, an area to have tea, coffee, and tea biscuits or cookies, and an endless supply of books and newspapers to read. One afternoon each week we get together and pass several hours in a "reader's heaven." If you haven't tried it, you should very soon. We recommend it highly.

Saturday January 20

WATCHING my great-grandchildren heading off to skate reminded me of this lovely poem by Gladys Harp.

Skating on the Pond

When winter days are short and cold,
Our warmest clothing donned,
We often take our ice skates out
And go skating on the pond.

The girls in bright-hued jackets
And the boys in Mackinaws,
Make as pretty a picture card
As any artist draws.
The ruddy sun sinking in the west
Paints a rosy glow
On the entire winter landscape,
Cloaked in ice and snow...
And if we stay till it is dark,
We build a bonfire bright
And gather round it now and then
To enjoy the flickering light.
The flames push back the edge of night,
And sparks soar ever higher
Each time somebody throws a log
Upon the smoldering fire.
We're making pictures for an album
Of memories beyond
Our youthful days in winter
Spent skating on the pond.

Sunday January 21

B E strong and of good courage; be not afraid,
neither be thou dismayed: for the Lord thy
God is with thee whithersoever thou goest.

Joshua 1:9

Monday January 22

YOU say God only exists because we believe in Him; but what if we only exist because He believes in us?

Tuesday January 23

MANY parents find it quite difficult when the last of their children leave home. The empty nest syndrome is something that all parents cope with in different ways. One of our neighbours, who recently became an empty nester when her youngest took an apartment of her own, found an interesting way to boost her sagging spirits. She made a list of things to enjoy now that she and her husband are alone again.

The salad doesn't have the olives picked out.
When the phone rings, it is for you.
No need to yell "shotgun" when you want a front seat in the car.
Rooms that are tidied, stay tidy.
You can watch television shows that you like.

Of course, these are exactly the same things that she misses!

Wednesday January 24

THE icy chill of today's wind reminded me of a story that my husband George and I followed with interest many years ago.

Back in 1934, the 46-year-old American Richard E. Byrd spent 4 1/2 months in isolation in the forbidding environment of the Ross Ice Barrier in the Antarctic.

The Rolling Advance Weather Base was set up to keep important weather records of the 4.5 million-square-mile Antarctic continent. At that time, the area was a meteorological blank. Byrd proposed to combine this data with data collected at "Little America," a base set up on the coast to reveal atmospheric conditions in the hemisphere.

Admiral Byrd survived temperatures as low as –80°F, carbon monoxide poisoning (from a faulty stovepipe), long months of blackness, and the psychological effects of isolation.

His survival and reports of his work are a lasting testament to human courage and endurance.

Thursday January 25
Robbie Burns Day

But pleasures are like poppies spread—
You seize the flow'r, its bloom is shed;
Or like the snowfalls in the river—
A moment white—then melts forever.

Friday January 26

NOSTALGIA is like an anaesthetic; You experience no pain, only a beautiful haze. When you grow older, what matters to you is not the way it was, but the way you remember it.

Roger and Natalie Whittaker

Saturday January 27

O give me the joy of living
And some glorious work to do;
A spirit of thanksgiving
With loyal heart and true;
Some pathway to make brighter
Where tired feet now stray;
Some burden to make lighter
While it is still day.

In the fields of the Master gleaning
May my hands and heart be strong;
May I know life's deepest meaning,
May I sing life's sweetest song;
With some faithful friends to love me,
May I always do my best;
And at last with heaven above me
Let me be at rest.

From an old Sunday school merit card

Sunday January 28

CAST thy burden upon the Lord, and He shall sustain thee: He shall never suffer the righteous to be moved.

Psalm 55:22

Monday January 29

ALTHOUGH a cure for the common cold has yet to be found, my grandson Marshall recounted a most interesting university study that says you can beat colds and flu just by sniffing chocolate.

A study in Britain revealed that people who sniffed the aroma of chocolate had a dramatic increase in immune system levels.

As Marshall explained, "Smelling chocolate apparently boosts the part of the immune system that protects you from colds, flu, respiratory infections or stomach bugs. According to the doctors who performed the research, you can benefit from sniffing chocolate six times a day for two seconds at a time. And that's not all, Gran. It seems that you can boost your immune system with other pleasant experiences like writing down a happy memory, or listening to your favourite song morning and night."

Hmm...I wonder if eating chocolate might also help!

Tuesday January 30

IT might take a while, but someday we learn that what we really are is all the experiences and all the thoughts we've ever had.

Wednesday January 31

MY son-in-law John made us laugh with this story today.

One Sunday morning an evangelist asked his congregation, "How many of you want to go to heaven?"

Everyone raised his or her hand except young Jimmy, who crossed his arms firmly across his chest and frowned.

"What about you, Jimmy?" the preacher asked incredulously. "Don't you want to go to heaven?"

"Well, yes, of course I do," young Jimmy answered. "I want to go sometime. I thought you were getting a group together to leave right now."

February

February

The fields are bedded down with snow
Like blankets tucked about their ears,
As if the world had gone to sleep.
But now and then a bush appears
Wearing a crown of purest gems,
With scarlet berries on white stems.

The windbreak running to the lake
Has snowy trunks like silver birch;
Even the weeds have hoods of snow,
Like quaint old women in a church.
The hens have frosted beards and look
Like old men in a picture book.

Along the highway muffled wheels
Go by without a breath of sound.
The fence posts stand like sentinels
Wearing tall helmets diamond crowned;
The mailman in his battered truck
Has drifted snow and ice to buck.

And yet I know that spring is nigh
Although the wind is cold and raw;
The sky is softer than it was,
The fields have started in to thaw,
Putting aside their winter dress
To don their springtime loveliness.

Edna Jacques

Friday February 2

TODAY is Groundhog Day, a day when the comings and goings of groundhogs are supposed to determine an early or a late spring.

According to tradition, if it sees its shadow, the groundhog returns to its hole for six more weeks of winter.

I, for one, am dearly hoping for a "shadowless" day. I am longing for the sunshine and days of warm weather!

Saturday February 3

My dear friend Muriel stopped by today. She is a "fishing widow" this weekend, her husband, Will, having gone ice fishing for the next few days. Long after the summer fishermen have stored away their tackle until spring, these hardy people get out their spuds, skimmers, buckets and tilts, and head for the bitterly cold, windswept ponds or lakes. For the life of me, I can not understand the mind that thinks it is a pleasant experience to sit for hours in frigid weather, wiggling a string hoping for a nibble or a bite.

Apparently Muriel thinks the way I do—she is inside a warm house with me.

Will seems to live by these words: "The Lord never deducts from a man's life span those hours spent fishing."

Sunday February 4

ALL people that on earth do dwell
Sing to the Lord with cheerful voice,
Him serve with mirth, His praise forth tell
Come ye before him and rejoice.

Scottish Psalter 1650

Monday February 5

MY former readers know that my very good friend Jake Frampton owns a small used bookstore. Knowing how much I enjoy reading, he brings me several books each time he comes to visit. Knowing also that mysteries are favourites of mine, today he brought me several works by Faye Kellerman and her husband, Jonathan Kellerman. I find it quite interesting that husband and wife should both be writers of mystery stories.

In fact, while Faye Kellerman has been exclusively a mystery writer, Jonathan had a distinguished career in child psychology. Although he now writes fiction full time, he is also the author of two volumes of psychology and a children's book. Each of these two authors offer books that are fast-paced, intelligent thrillers. I anticipate several late nights of reading.

Tuesday February 6

IT is a curious fact that of all the illusions that beset mankind, none is quite so curious as that tendency to suppose that we are mentally and morally superior to those who differ from us in opinion.

Elbert Hubbard

Wednesday February 7

SHARED laughter creates a bond of friendship. When people laugh together, they cease to be young and old, master and pupils, worker and driver. They have become a single group of human beings, enjoying their existence.

W. Grant Lee

Thursday February 8

MANY things which cannot be overcome when they are together, yield themselves up when taken little by little.

Plutarch

Sometimes, when we are faced with a seemingly overwhelming amount to do, it helps if we begin to do it one small bit at a time. Soon we find that we have accomplished much more than we thought possible—and maybe worried about it less.

Friday February 9

MY grandson Marshall has a sense of humour that has always appealed greatly to me. He seems to be able to find humour in so many different places. Today he offered a list of actual label instructions on consumer goods (along with appropriate comments).

On a Sears hairdryer—
"Do not use while sleeping."
(Gosh, that's the only time I have to work on my hair!)

On a bag of Fritos—
"You could be a winner! No purchase necessary. Details inside."
(Would this be a shoplifter's special?)

On Boots cough medicine for children—
"Do not drive a car or operate machinery after taking this medication."
(Perhaps there would be fewer construction accidents if we could keep those 5-year-olds with head colds off the forklifts.)

On Nytol sleep aid—
"Warning: May cause drowsiness."
(One would hope!)

On most brands of Christmas lights—
"For indoor or outdoor use only."
(As opposed to what?)

Saturday February 10

The future lies before you
Like a field of driven snow,
Be careful how you tread it,
For every step will show.

Sunday February 11

THOUGH God has never been seen by any man, God himself dwells in us if we love one another; His love is brought to perfection within us.

I John 4:12

Monday February 12

ABRAHAM Lincoln was not particularly handsome. Someone once remarked that he was a very common-looking man, to which Lincoln replied, "Friend, the Lord prefers common-looking people. That is the reason He makes so many of them."

Who could have guessed that this "common-looking man" would be an uncommonly brilliant president of the United States?

In dedicating the military cemetery at Gettysburg, Lincoln said "…that this nation, under God, shall have a new birth of freedom—and that government of the people, by the people, for the people, shall not perish from the earth."

Tuesday February 13

NO one person can help everyone, but everyone can help one person.

Wednesday February 14
Valentine's Day

ST. Valentine's Day is a day that is special in many countries around the world. Here in North America, we celebrate in a multitude of ways. Cards, flowers, candy and gifts are a few of the ways that you can tell someone how much you care.

St. Valentine was a Christian martyr who died in the third century. It is thought that the celebration of St. Valentine probably derived from the ancient Roman Feast of Lupercalia, which was held on February 15. On that day it was the custom for young men and maidens to draw partners for the coming year. As the number of Christians increased in the empire, Lupercalia became linked to the feast St. Valentine held on February 14. So it was that St. Valentine became known as the patron saint of lovers.

Love is like magic
And it always will be,
For love still remains
Life's sweet mystery.

Helen Steiner Rice

Thursday February 15

I FIRMLY believe that any man's finest hour, his greatest fulfillment of all he holds dear, is that moment when he has worked his heart out in a good cause and lies exhausted on the field of battle…victorious.

Vince Lombardi

Friday February 16

NO man or woman of the humblest sort can really be strong, gentle, pure, and good without the world being better for it, without somebody being helped and comforted by the very existence of that goodness.

Phillip Brooks

Saturday February 17

WHEN I get up each morning, I like to remember that every new day holds a new beginning. Even if yesterday did not embrace the success that we wished for, today gives us another chance to accomplish our goals.

Great works are performed, not by strength, but by perseverance.

Goethe

Sunday February 18

AND the Lord, He it is that doth go before thee, He will be with thee, He will not fail thee, neither forsake thee: fear not, neither be dismayed.

Deuteronomy 31:8

Monday February 19

MY great-granddaughter Jenny stopped in to see me today. We enjoyed some hot chocolate and sugar cookies while we talked about her school activities, her friends and then, the family.

"You know Gran, I really don't understand some of my friends. They fight with their parents all the time; they say mean things about their brothers and sisters; I don't get it. Justin and I don't always agree about everything but he is my very best friend, and I wouldn't think of saying something nasty about him to anyone else. And

Mom and Dad sometimes get angry with Justin and me, but they have never treated us with anything but love and kindness, and I can't imagine my life in constant conflict with them. I feel so lucky to have the family that I have!"

And so do I, my dear—so do I!

Tuesday February 20

ABOUT a year and a half ago dear friends of mine, Don and Joan Kepron, tragically lost one of their five sons, Kevin. The loss of a child is so difficult, so hard to accept. This morning I came across the transcript of the eulogy to Kevin, and I share part of it with you today.

"When someone lives a full life, to an old age, and then passes away, we somehow find acceptance of their loss easier. When life is cut short, in its prime, at the time that it should be hitting its stride, it seems incomprehensible. We can look for answers but ... in the end maybe it's not so much that we have to understand it, but rather that we find a place to put it, to make peace with it in our lives.

Kevin was so smart, so full of promise. He was crafty and creative. He was a perfectionist in an imperfect world. He was intense, boisterous, emotional, curious.

We cannot make the mistake of dwelling in darkness, of permanently surrendering to sorrow, of living with regrets and 'what ifs,' or 'if onlys.' We owe it to ourselves, to Kevin, to God, to live with grace in the aftermath of this loss. We have been changed forever because of it, because of Kevin's life and death. We have come together, as family, with a stronger and deeper sense of what it means to be 'family,' to love and to embrace life.

God bless us all."

Kevin, you are missed and not forgotten.

Wednesday February 21

WE are here to help each other, to try to make each other happy.

Saying of the Inuit

How wise we would be to heed those words. Too often, we can become self-centred and self-focussed, wondering what others can do for us, when we really should be thinking about how we can help others. For it's in helping others that we most help ourselves.

Thursday February 22

MEN go abroad to wonder at the height of the mountains, at the huge waves of the sea, at the long courses of the rivers, at the vast compass of the ocean, at the circular motion of the stars; and they pass by themselves without wondering.

St. Augustine

Friday February 23

ICONSIDER a human soul without education like marble in the quarry, which shows none of its inherent beauties till the skill of the polisher fetches out the colours, makes the surface shine, and discovers every ornamental cloud, spot, and vein that runs through the body of it.

Joseph Addison

Saturday February 24

HEARING my great-grandsons talk about their day at the ski hills brought to mind this lovely poem by Grace Noll Crowell:

Ski Heights

Here where an echo is as thin
As clear blown glass, a cry rings out;
Here where the skiers late have been,
There is nothing left but an echoing shout
As the last man follows a piled white trail,
Skimming the surface as light as foam,
Swaying and tilting—an eager sail,
Set for some far wild winter home.

Bereft, the heights take on new light:
The cold blue quivers as ardent red
Flows where the sun, before the night,
Banks its coals for the day ahead.
And the lonely heights now wait and dream
Of laughter and shouting, of youth, a thrill—
Of morning when white frosts glitter and gleam,
And the skiers once more take to the hill.

Sunday February 25

Rock of ages, cleft for me,
Let me hide myself in thee;
Let the water and the Blood
From the riven side which flowed,
Be of sin the double cure,
Clease me from its guilt and power.

One of the most popular hymns of all time, "Rock of Ages" was composed under most unusual circumstances. It was written in 1775 by Augustus Toplady at Barrington Coombe, in Somerset, England.

During a storm, he took shelter in the cleft of a large rock. To pass the time while waiting for the rain to stop, he wrote the famous song on a playing card.

After an unorthodox beginning, this remains one of the most beloved of all hymns.

Monday February 26

WHEN the day returns, call us up with morning faces and with morning hearts, eager to labour, happy if happiness be our portion and if the day be marked for sorrow, strong to endure.

Robert Louis Stevenson

Tuesday February 27

WE are nearing the end of February and the celebration of Black History Month in Canada. Originally observed as Negro History Week when it began in the United States in 1926, February was chosen because it was the birth month of both U.S. President Abraham Lincoln and Frederick Douglas, a Maryland-born former slave.

His book, "Narrative of the Life of Frederick Douglas," stirred sympathy in the north for escaped slaves.

Canada played a unique role in the history of Black America. Our country was the end of the underground railway, a prearranged route along which fleeing slaves could travel north to Canada. It's estimated that some 30,000 slaves escaped as a result of the underground railway.

Many of the men, women and children who arrived in Canada made their home in Elgin Settlement, in North Buxton, near Chatham,

Ontario. Today, the Elgin settlement is one of the few remaining African-Canadian settlements that have been in existence since pre–Civil War days. Today, the settlement is inhabited, for the most part, by descendents of the original settlers who chose to remain in Canada. There is a museum in North Buxton that was opened as a memorial to the Elgin Settlement. Much emphasis is placed upon the history and accomplishments of the original settlers.

It is well worth a visit!

Wednesday February 28
Ash Wednesday

A S we begin the season of Lent, I feel it is a time for self-examination—a day for beginning afresh some resolve to grow in faith, to renew our hope and discover new ways of expressing the love we experience through our community of believers.

Many of the older customs associated with Lent have changed. From a senior's point of view the new ideas are more open and challenging. They provide fresh thoughts about an ancient faith. May we use these 40 days as a time of renewal.

March

Thursday March 1

ON this first day of March, many Bulgarian-Canadians follow an interesting Old World custom. Small tokens made of red and white thread are worn pinned to the lapel. "Marteniki," as they are called, used to be small pieces of white and red thread that were twisted together. They were thrown outdoors for the storks or swallows to use in making their nests. This tradition continues today here in Canada, and the "marteniki" are often offered to the first robins of spring.

Friday March 2

AS we come into a month that we hope will give us better weather, we need to be aware of the drivers who choose to use improved road conditions as an excuse to speed. Our minister had an idea for highway signs giving posted speed limits.

At 100 kph, "You'll take the high road and I'll take the low road."

At 110 kph," Guide me, O thou great Jehovah."

At 120 kph, "Nearer my God to thee."

At 130 kph, "When the roll is called up yonder, I'll be there."

Saturday March 3

I SHARED a visit today at the home of a younger friend, Bonnie Gosse. Bonnie is one of those rare people who is always a joy to be around. She is kind, cheerful—a person who handles all that life sends her with a calm acceptance and a happy outlook. Her house is decorated with angels because she has a great faith in the power of her belief in "guardian angels." These lines, from an unknown author, are some of her favourites.

All I Need To Know About Life I Learned From My Guardian Angel

Know all the possibilities of your impossible dream.

Leave space in your relationships so you'll have lots of time to play.

Be yourself.

Forgive, forget and forge ahead.

It's easier to fly when you take yourself lightly.

Reach out and touch someone lightly with your wings.

Love is the only four letter word you know.

It's okay to cry during movies.
Don't postpone joy to scrub the bathroom or clean the garage.
Love Mother Earth.
Whenever you feel afraid, call a friend.
Carry a spare set of wings in your pocket.
Wherever you go is where you will be.
Spread your wings and fly.

Sunday March 4

O LORD, who for our sake did'st fast forty days and forty nights; Give us grace to use such abstinence, that, our flesh being subdued to the Spirit, we may ever obey thy godly motions in righteousness, and true holiness, to thy honour and glory, who livest and reignest with the Father and the Holy Ghost, one God, world without end. Amen.

Collect for the first Sunday in Lent

Monday March 5

T HERE are two ways of spreading light: to be the candle or the mirror that reflects it.

Edith Wharton

Tuesday March 6

LITERATURE is not an abstract science, to which exact definitions can be applied. It is an art, the success of which depends on personal persuasiveness, on the author's skill to give as well as on ours to receive,

Sir Arthur Thomas Quiller-Couch

Wednesday March 7

I CAME across an old photo album today and was almost overwhelmed by the memories that flooded back on seeing the bygone pictures.

Many years ago, my husband, George, and I spent one winter in Montreal. What I remember most from that time are the sleighs. No other city in Canada had such a rich variety of commercial sleighs—the coal man's, the "frites" or chip sleighs, the fruit and vegetable peddler's sleigh, the rag picker's sleigh, and many more.

Most Montrealers with cars usually put them up on blocks because it was much too difficult to maneuver down the snow-banked streets. The old horse-drawn sleigh had the run of the roads!

The fruit and vegetable peddler's sleigh was unique. It was usually heated by an old Quebec coal-burning stove, and it had a tiny chimney on the roof.

Another of my favourites was the "frites" sleigh. I can almost taste those delicious French-fried potatoes served in a paper cone with vinegar and lots of salt.

Seeing those faded photos brought back many happy memories of an era I had almost forgotten.

Thursday March 8

IN Canada, we women regard our right to vote and participate in government as a natural part of our democratic system. This was not always so, and indeed, in many countries around the world, equality for women is just a dream.

International Women's Day, on March 8, is a day set aside for us to express our concerns about inequality in women's rights worldwide. Although we here in Canada have made significant advancements toward equality, there remain many areas for improvement.

I was interested to learn why March 8 was selected, and found that it is the anniversary of the first march, held in New York City in 1857, to protest the appalling conditions for women in the textile industry.

Not that long ago in Canada, women didn't have the right to vote—now they are members of parliament and cabinet ministers. We do make progress!

Friday March 9

ONE of the hardest things to teach children about money matters is that it does.

Saturday March 10

WHEN we walk to the edge of all the light we have and take a step into the darkness of the unknown, we must believe that one of two things will happen: there will be something solid for us to stand on…or…God will teach us to fly.

Author unknown

Sunday March 11

ETERNAL God, our hearts are restless until they rest in you. Let your glory shine on us, that our lives may proclaim your goodness, our work give you honour and our voices praise you forever, for the sake of Jesus Christ our Lord.

Book of Alternative Services

Monday March 12

NOTHING changes more constantly than the past; for the past that influences our lives does not consist of what actually happened, but of what men believe happened.

Gerald White Johnson

Tuesday March 13

IT has been almost five years now since Erma Bombeck, beloved American humourist, passed away. As I reread her books, I am still amused by her rib-tickling wisdom and marvel at her incredible ability to make us laugh at ourselves. For more than three decades, she was a nationally syndicated humour columnist and author of numerous best-selling books. Today, I offer a few of Erma's hilarious observations:

It's frightening to wake up one morning and discover that while you were asleep, you went out of style.

I have just come up with a wonderful solution on how to end all wars. Let men give the directions on how to get there.

The hippopotamus is a vegetarian and looks like a wall. Lions, who eat only red meat, are sleek and slim. Are nutritionists on the wrong track?

My second favourite household chore is ironing. My first is hitting my head on the top bunk until I faint.

I cook enough spaghetti to feed Sicily and no one shows. I make two small pieces of leftover pizza for dinner and they fly in from out of state!

Wednesday March 14

It is the first mild day of March:
Each minute sweeter than before,
The redbreast sings from the tall larch
That stands beside our door.

There is a blessing in the air,
Which seems a sense of joy to yield
To the bare trees, and mountains bare,
And grass in the green field.

William Wordsworth

I saw my first robin today and it lifted my spirits immeasurably. My daughter Julia and I were looking out the window when the robin landed in our yard. If a robin has returned, can spring be far behind?

Thursday March 15

IF a man has a talent and cannot use it, he has failed. If he has a talent and uses only half of it, he has partly failed. If he has a talent and learns somehow to use the whole of it, he has gloriously succeeded, and won a satisfaction and a triumph few men can ever know.

Thomas Wolfe

Friday March 16

MY son-in-law John is a minister in the Anglican Church. I always enjoy time spent with John and my daughter Mary because their lives so closely parallel my own with my husband, George. John finds his many dinner meetings as onerous as did George, although there really is little choice but to attend, because each group's agenda is important in the life of the church.

Whenever John and Mary come for dinner, I try to have a meal that I hope will be a little different from the too-oft served "chicken specials" that John has to eat so frequently.

This evening I offered a roast of lamb, boiled, parsleyed new potatoes, "company" carrots and the pièce de résistance—chocolate cheesecake.

There is something so heartwarming about serving a meal to an appreciative guest. John raved, smacked his lips and offered so many "Mmmm, delicious" comments that I lost count. Whenever I require a boost in spirits, I need only invite John and Mary for dinner. John makes me feel like a gourmet chef!

Saturday March 17
St. Patrick's Day

MAY you be in heaven an hour before the devil knows you are gone.

Irish Proverb

Sunday March 18

WE beseech thee, Almighty God, look upon the hearty desires of thy humble servants, and stretch forth the right hand of thy majesty, to be our defense against all our enemies; through Jesus Christ our Lord. Amen.

Collect for the third Sunday in Lent

Monday March 19

SOME people are blessed with an even temperament and are rarely upset by life's little problems. For those of us who are not so lucky and have a temper that is a little quicker to rise, I offer Margaret Sangster's view of losing one's temper.

"It's like a sharp nail that tears the threads of something durable and lovely. We may use every bit of our patience and skill in mending it, but we cannot make it like new again. The darned place will always be conspicuous."

Tuesday March 20

A PESSIMIST is one who makes difficulties of his opportunities; an optimist is one who makes opportunities of his difficulties.

Wednesday March 21

WHAT lovelier way to begin spring than with these words of joy:

For lo, the winter is past, the rain is over and gone; The flowers appear the on earth; the time of the singing of birds is come, and the voice of the turtle is heard in our land.

The Song of Solomon 2:11–12

Thursday March 22

The Spring

Now that the winter's gone, the earth hath lost
Her snow-white robes; and now no more the frost
Candies the grass, or casts an icy cream
Upon the silver lake or crystal stream;
But the warm sun thaws the benumbèd earth,
And makes it tender; gives a sacred birth
To the dead swallow; wakes in hollow tree
The drowsy cuckoo and the humblebee.
Now do a choir of chirping minstrels bring,
In triumph to the world, the youthful spring.

Thomas Carew

Friday March 23

It takes more grace than man can tell
To play the second fiddle well.

Saturday March 24

L AST evening some friends and I watched the Oscar-winning documentary movie, "The Silent World," filmed by Jacques Yves Cousteau. I was so fascinated by the film that I set out to learn more about the genius who was Jacques Cousteau.

Born near Bordeaux, France, in 1910, Cousteau aspired to be a navy aviator, until a near-fatal car crash put an end to that dream. When he took up swimming to strengthen his arms after the crash, he found his true calling—the sea. He would later write, "Sometimes we are lucky enough to know that our lives have been changed, to discard the old, embrace the new and run headlong down an immutable course. It happened to me on that summer's day when my eyes were opened by the sea."

Before Cousteau, divers were limited by the length of their breath, or the tether on the diving helmet. His co-invention of the aqualung allows us to roam the ocean as never before.

In 1950, Cousteau acquired a 66-foot minesweeper named the *Calypso*, which he turned into a floating oceanographic laboratory. He would sail her around the world for more than four decades. Although Captain Cousteau passed away in 1997 at the age of 87, he has left us a legacy in films, books and the "Cousteau Society," founded in 1973 and operating today under the guidance of his family. He opened wonders of the oceans to us as no one has done before or since.

Sunday March 25

Lord, as to thy dear Cross we flee,
And plead to be forgiven,
So let thy life our pattern be,
And form our souls for heaven.

Canon J. H. Gurney, Anglican Hymn Book

Monday March 26

THE whole difference between construction and creation is exactly this: that a thing constructed can only be loved after it is constructed; but a thing created can be loved before it exists.

Gilbert Keith Chesterton

Tuesday Marsh 27

WHY is it that, when you have a choice of chocolates and bite into one, it's never the right one?

Wednesday March 28

THIS is the time of year in many areas when the sap is collected from the maple trees to make that delicious treat, maple syrup. It used to be that the trees were tapped individually and sap collected in buckets. Children were often given time off from school to help with the drilling of holes, the collecting of sap, and the boiling down process known as sugaring off.

Since that time, progress has been made. The process of collecting sap has been modified, and now plastic hoses bring the sap from each tree to one large holding tank.

In Quebec, the sugaring off is known as the "Festival de la cabane à sucre."

On Canada's east coast these sugaring off parties are called "licheries." My sister Sarah and her husband, Richard, called this evening to tell me of the licherie that they attended today.

"We had a wonderful time, Edna. The syrup was boiled just to the point of turning to toffee, and then it was scooped up on a big stick. Each of us scraped off our share on a little palette. Most of us licked the syrup like candy."

I can recollect eating the syrup with salt cod and roasted potatoes. My mouth is fairly watering as I remember that treat.

Thursday March 29

MY friend Jake remarked today that one problem with living in a small town is that your house is always known by the name of the people who lived there before.

Friday March 30

BOOKS are the treasured wealth of the world and the fit inheritance of generations and nations ... Their authors are a natural and irresistible aristocracy in every society, and, more than kings or emperors, exert an influence on mankind.

Henry David Thoreau

Saturday March 31

NOTHING worth doing is completed in our lifetime; therefore, we must be saved by hope. Nothing true or beautiful or good makes complete sense in any immediate context of history; therefore we must be saved by faith. Nothing we do, however virtuous, can be accomplished alone; therefore, we are saved by love.

Reinhold Niebuhr

April

Sunday April 1

WE beseech thee, Almighty God, mercifully to look upon thy people; that by thy great goodness they may be governed and preserved evermore, both in body and soul; through Jesus Christ our Lord. Amen.

Collect for the fifth Sunday in Lent

Monday April 2

I thank the unknown author for these lines on "Priceless Things."

Life holds so many priceless things ...
The falling rain—the wind that sings,
Each star on high—a big full moon,
And sunbeams dancing bright in June,
The river as it rushes on,
A sunset when the day is gone;
No wealth can buy a mountain tall
These priceless things belong to all.
An autumn tree lends beauty rare
With coloured leaves most everywhere;
As nature wears a glowing smile

Making every day worthwhile.
Could anything be quite as dear
As laughing children that we hear?
The gift of friendship that is ours,
The miracle of growing flowers,
Each magic moment—treasured time,
These priceless gifts are yours and mine.

Tuesday April 3

OPPORTUNITIES are never lost. Someone else takes those you miss.

Wednesday April 4

I NEVER cease to be amazed by advancements made in science and technology. Some heart surgery is now performed by a robot—an amazing machine that allows doctors to operate with greater accuracy than ever before. A doctor controls the machine much like those of a video game.

The surgeon sits at a console where he can see everything on a computer screen. The three-armed robot has one voice-activated arm with a camera to provide accurate viewing. The other two arms manipulate surgical instruments and perform the surgeon's moves with computer enhanced precision, as he moves the joysticks. It is thought that patients with cardiovascular disease may do better with these less invasive surgical procedures.

For someone like me, who still has trouble comprehending the workings of the telephone, this robot is mind boggling.

Thursday April 5

GEORGE Bernard Shaw probably spoke for many of us when he described his behaviour during a crisis.

"In moments of crisis, my nerves act in a most extraordinary way. When disaster seems imminent, my whole being is simultaneously braced to avoid it. I size up the situation in a flash, set my teeth, contract my muscles, take a firm grip of myself, and without a tremor, always do the wrong thing."

Friday April 6

I TOOK advantage of the spring-like weather today to take my friend Lila for a walk in her wheelchair. Lila and I both enjoy our neighbourhood walks so much—me for the exercise and Lila for the opportunity to leave her nursing home and the pleasure of seeing spring come to raise her spirits.

Today, we passed the house where Lila used to live with her husband and family. Many people might have been saddened to see the changes that the new owners have made. Not Lila. She spoke with such enthusiasm about the new porch, the colour changes to doors and windows, the new walkway.

"Why Edna, isn't it wonderful! To think our old house could look so beautiful. It makes me so happy!"

Saturday April 7

YOU know, we never know how the little things we do for others will help in ways that we can't imagine. I was reminded of this when I answered my doorbell this morning. On the front step was a smiling young man holding a pot of daffodils.

"Mrs. McCann, these are for you."

Although he looked somewhat familiar, I didn't recognize him until he spoke his name. I invited him inside and he told me his story.

"You used to come to our school every week to help some of us with our reading. I don't know how well you may remember me but I was a terrible reader! I didn't like to read and I was very embarrassed because I read so poorly. You helped to change that for me.

"At first you read to me but then gradually you encouraged me to pick out the words that I knew. You would tell me every day what a clever boy I was, and eventually I began to believe you. Soon I was reading as well as everyone else in my class—I even learned to love reading.

"I have just graduated from university and I wanted to give you these flowers as a thank you. I believe that you made it possible for me!"

Sunday April 8
Palm Sunday
Ride on! Ride on in majesty!
Hark! All the tribes hosanna cry;
O Saviour meek, pursue the road
With palms and scattered garments strowed.

Ride on! Ride on in majesty!
In lowly pomp ride on to die;
O Christ, thy triumphs now begin
O'er captive death and conquered sin.

Hymn for Palm Sunday, Dean H. H. Milman

Monday April 9
TO own a bit of ground, to scratch it with a hoe, to plant seeds, and watch the renewal of life—this is the commonest delight of the race, the most satisfactory thing a man can do.

Charles Dudley Warner

I believe those words were written especially for my brother, Ben. There is nothing that he loves to do more than gardening, and he does it all year round. In winter, he spends time in his basement hothouse area, nurturing seeds into plants that he will put in the garden in spring. As well, he researches seed catalogues as one would study the works of the masters. For him, gardening is "the most satisfactory thing a man can do."

Tuesday April 10

OLIVER Wendell Holmes once offered this good advice:

"Don't flatter yourself that friendship authorizes you to say disagreeable things to your intimates. On the contrary, the nearer you come into relationship with a person, the more necessary do fact and courtesy become. Except in cases of necessity, which are rare, let your friend learn unpleasant truths from his enemies—they are usually ready to tell him."

Wednesday April 11

MARG and I came out of the restaurant after lunch today and were surprised to see a young woman sitting in the driver's seat of Marg's car. Seeing us looking at her, she opened the door and in a voice filled with frustration announced:

"I don't know what on earth is wrong with this key. It won't start my car!"

Marg started to laugh, and we both noticed, at the same time, an identical car parked beside ours.

"I think you'll find your car next to this one, which is mine." Marg pointed out.

The poor girl was so embarrassed, but she finally laughed as hard as we did, and waved as she drove off—in her own car.

Thursday April 12

YOUR true character is what shows after the spotlight has been turned off, the applause has died down, and no one is around to give you credit.

Friday April 13
Good Friday

ALMIGHTY God, look graciously we pray, on this your family for whom our Lord, Jesus Christ, was willing to be betrayed and given into the hands of sinners and to suffer death upon the cross, who now lives and reigns with you and the Holy Spirit, one God, for ever and ever. Amen.

The Book of Common Prayer

Saturday April 14

MY friend Will, our local "gardener extraordinaire," designed a lovely surprise for our neighbourhood, way last fall. Knowing that Easter was later in April this year, he planted crocus bulbs on his front lawn. To our delight, his flowers are blooming and spelling out "Happy Easter" for all to see.

Sunday April 15

FOR me, Easter is the loveliest day of the year. The spiritual lift I get from the Easter service leaves me with a sense of renewed strength of faith, and belief in the life to come.

It was with great joy that I sang this morning,
Christ the Lord is risen today
Sons of Men and angels say;
Raise your joys and triumphs high;
Sing, ye heavens; thou earth reply.

Rev. Charles Wesley

Monday April 16

THOSE who bring sunshine to the lives of others cannot keep it from themselves.

J. M. Barrie

I think often of these words when I see the many volunteers who work at our local nursing home. It's so easy to tell that their kind words or comforting hugs given to the elderly residents bring great pleasure to them. The volunteers seem to share in the glow of the happiness they bring. They are true treasures!

Tuesday April 17

MY friend Mavis Tewbury, who lives in Winnipeg, wrote to me of a most interesting few days that she recently spent in Saskatchewan.

"The Saskatchewan Indian Federated College

is located in Regina. This school is the only First-Nations controlled, university-level college in Canada. This beautiful college offers both under-graduate and graduate degree opportunities within the environment of First Nations' cultural affirmation. The school hires its own faculty and staff and offers academic programs from a unique First Nations' perspective. Contact with elders also enhances the life of students at the college. The elders (three men and two women) are respected for their spirituality and provide a link to the traditional ways of the First Nations.

Each spring the college hosts a powwow cele-bration, and I was lucky enough to attend with my friends Betty and Don. It was quite spectac-ular. There were dancers from all across North America, and we watched for hours as they performed traditional dances. As well, there were exquisite native crafts and delicious tradi-tional foods to be sampled. I brought home several lovely dreamcatchers for my grandchil-dren. It was a wonderful time for all of us."

Wednesday April 18

SPRING and early summer bring a delicious treat that many of you may not be familiar with. Fiddleheads are the unopened fronds of fiddlehead ferns, which can be cooked and served as a vegetable or used in salads. They can be found in most supermarkets and many specialty markets.

Fiddleheads with Lemon Butter

1 lb. fiddleheads
2 tbsp. melted butter
juice of one lemon
salt & pepper to taste.

Wash the fiddleheads carefully so as not to break them. Place washed fiddleheads in boiling water. Boil 5–6 minutes or until tender. Drain. Place in serving dish. Melt butter. Squeeze the juice from the lemon in to the melted butter. Pour over the fiddleheads and toss lightly.

Fiddleheads are also wonderful in a salad. Wash, then place them in boiling water. Cook until tender. Drain and refrigerate until chilled. They are a delicious way to enhance a chef's salad or jellied vegetable salad.

Thursday April 19
O! How this spring of love resembleth
The certain glory of an April day!

William Shakespeare

Friday April 20

THIS is also the time of year when our friends of the Jewish faith celebrate Pesach or Passover. Passover is the festival of freedom to commemorate the exodus of the Israelites from Egypt. It is a time of family gatherings and lavish meals called Seders, where the story of the Passover is retold through the reading of the Haggadah, the book of Exodus.

The Seder, the most important event in the Passover celebration, is both a meal and a service of worship. The Seder table is set with special dishes used just for this event, as families celebrate this very important Jewish festival.

My I wish to all of my Jewish friends a joyous Passover.

Saturday April 21

EVERY heart that has beat strong and cheerfully has left a hopeful impulse behind it in the world, and bettered the tradition of mankind.

Robert Louis Stevenson

Sunday April 22

Be truthful, be steadfast, whatever betide thee,
Only one thing do thou ask the Lord,
Grace to go forward wherever he guide thee,
Simply believing the truth of his word.

Monday April 23

WRITE it on your heart that every day is the best day in the year.

Ralph Waldo Emerson

Tuesday April 24

AS I walked beside the millpond today I noticed that the trilliums were just beginning to poke out of the ground. The white trillium, of course, is Ontario's floral emblem. Did you ever wonder what flowers the other provinces and territories chose?

Alberta	wild prickly rose
British Columbia	western flowering dogwood
Manitoba	prairie crocus
New Brunswick	purple violet
Newfoundland	pitcher plant
Nova Scotia	Mayflower
Ontario	white trillium
Prince Edward Island	pink lady's slipper
Quebec	Madonna lily
Saskatchewan	prairie red lily
Northwest Territories	mountain avens
Nunavut	Arctic poppy
Yukon Territories	fireweed

Wednesday April 25

ONE of the loveliest poems I have ever read
was written by Margaret Fishback Powers.
Originally titled "I Had a Dream," we now know
it as "Footprints."

One night I dreamed a dream.
I was walking along the beach with my Lord.
Across the dark sky flashed scenes from my life.
For each scene, I noticed two sets
of footprints in the sand,
one belonging to me
and one to my Lord.
When the last scene of my life shot before me
I looked back at the footprints in the sand.
There was only one set of footprints.
I realized that this was at the lowest
and saddest times of my life.
This always bothered me
and I questioned the Lord
about my dilemma.
"Lord, you told me when I decided to follow
    You,
You would walk and talk with me all the way.
But I'm aware that during the most trouble-
    some
times of my life there is only one set of foot-
    prints.
I just don't understand why, when I needed
    You most,

You leave me."
He whispered, "My precious child,
I love you and will never leave you
never, ever, during your trials and testings.
When you saw only one set of footprints
it was then that I carried you."

Thursday April 26

I GREW up on Canada's east coast and many the night I would hear a foghorn's mournful sound as it warned the incoming boats of danger. I thought that you might be interested to hear the story of the foghorn's invention.

Robert Foulis, of Saint John, New Brunswick, was walking home in a dense fog. Because he could not see, he had to listen to get his bearings.

It was then that he heard the sounds of his young daughter's piano playing. To his great surprise as he approached his home, it seemed as if she were playing only one note, low in the bass. Then it came to him that this was the only note in her music that had pierced the fog.

From this knowledge he invented the steam foghorn.

Friday April 27

I've heard it said that money talks,
The very thought intrigues me,

Mine never stops to have a chat
So hastily it leaves me.

Lola Sneyd

Saturday April 28

For memory has painted this beautiful day
With colours that never fade,
And we find at the end of a perfect day
The soul of a friend we've made.

Carrie Jacob Bonds

Sunday April 29

YE are the light of the world. A city that is set on a hill cannot be hid.

Neither do men light a candle, and put it under a bushel, but on a candlestick; and it giveth light unto all that are in the house.

Let your light so shine before men, that they may see your good works, and glorify your Father, which is in Heaven.

Matthew 5:14–16

Monday April 30

IWANT to sing like the birds sing, not worry-ing about who hears or what they think.

Rumi

May

Tuesday May 1

THIS lovely work from Sara Teasdale is still one of my favourites for this month of May.

May Day

A delicate fabric of bird song
Floats in the air,
The smell of wet wild earth
Is everywhere.

Red small leaves of the maple
Are clenched like a hand,
Like girls at their first communion
The pear trees stand.

Oh, I must pass nothing by
Without loving it much,
The raindrops try with my lips,
The grass with my touch;

For how can I be sure
I shall see again
The world on the first of May
Shining after the rain?

Wednesday May 2

MY son-in-law Bruce heard this next story on the radio several weeks ago. I thought that you might enjoy it as much as I did.

Near midnight, on Valentine's Day back in 1965, an older African-American lady was standing on the side of a highway in Alabama. It was a dreadful night—teeming rain—and her car had broken down. Soaking wet and desperately in need of a ride, she flagged down the next car to come along. A young white man stopped to assist her, an act that was pretty well unheard of in the American south during those years of racial conflict. The young man drove her into the city, made sure that she had help and put her in a cab to the airport so that she could catch her flight to Los Angeles. Rushed as she was, she wrote down the name and address of her benefactor.

A week later he was surprised to receive, at his home, a combination console television and stereo record player with this note attached.

Dear Mr. James,

Thank you so much for assisting me on the highway the other night. The rain drenched not only my clothes, but also my spirits. Then you came along. Because of you, I was able to make it to my dying husband's bedside just before he passed away. God bless you for helping me and unselfishly serving others.

Sincerely,
Mrs. Nat King Cole

Thursday May 3

ERNEST Hemingway once wrote, "If you are lucky enough to have lived in Paris as a young man, then wherever you go for the rest of your life, it stays with you, for Paris is a moveable feast."

My friend Emily recently returned from a trip to Paris and she wrote rapturously about it in her letter to me.

"Edna, Paris, was everything that I dreamed it would be!—city of lights—I can't begin to describe how much I enjoyed it. From the Champs Élysées with its fabulous stores and restaurants, the Eiffel Tower, the Louvre with its magnificent works of art, to the *bateaux mouches* on the Seine and the area of Montmartre—I loved it all."

I hope to enjoy her trip vicariously when she shows me her photos. Sometimes we can live the trip while staying here at home.

Travel, in the younger sort, is a part of education; in the elder, a part of experience.

Francis Bacon

He that travels far, knows much.

Clarke, 1639

Friday May 4

MIRTH is God's medicine. Everybody ought to bathe in it. Grim-care, moroseness, anxiety—all this rust of life ought to be scoured off by the oils of mirth. A man without mirth is like a wagon without springs, in which everyone is caused disagreeably to jolt by every pebble over which it runs.

Henry Ward Beecher

Saturday May 5

LIFE may be like a game of cards; we cannot help the hand we are dealt but we can help the way we play it.

Bishop Fulton Sheen

Sunday May 6

Rest of the weary,
Joy of the sad,
Hope of the dreary,
Light of the glad,
Home of the stranger,
Strength to the end,
Refuge from danger,
Saviour and friend.

Rev. J. S. B. Monsell

Monday May 7

MY grandson Marshall's wife, Jamie, has a wonderful sense of humour. She made me laugh with these unusual résumé inclusions—found on actual applications.

Let's meet so you can "ooh" and "aah" over my experience.

References: None. I've left a path of destruction behind me.

I'd like to be a sports writer. However, since I possess no training in journalism, I suppose I could try filing clerk.

I think that it is best for my employers that I not work with people.

You will want me to be head honcho in no time!

Tuesday May 8

ST. Francis of Assisi was hoeing his garden when a friend asked him what he would do if he learned that he was to die at sunset.

The reply? "I would finish hoeing my garden."

Wednesday May 9

A swarm of bees in May
Is worth a load of hay;
A swarm of bees in June
Is worth a silver spoon;
A swarm of bees in July
Is not worth a fly.

Old English Proverb

Thursday May 10

THIS is the time of year when many universities hold their commencement exercises. Students, watched by proud family members and friends, receive the graduation diplomas for which they worked so hard.

At the graduation exercises at St. Lawrence University several years ago, one young lady may have expressed the thoughts of many graduates on that day. Written in bold white letters on her mortarboard it said: "Don't Make Me Leave."

Friday May 11

WHEN others see but the dawn coming over the hill, I see the soul of God shouting for joy.

William Blake

Saturday May 12

My son-in-law Bruce and my grandson Marshall spent this day in a "winter's over, summer's coming" cleanup around the house. It was good of Marshall to give his dad a hand and they really enjoyed their day together. Bruce has quite a list of chores that he thinks should be done at this time of year. I wonder if you can add to the list.

Close the chimney flue.
Replace the furnace filters.
Inspect the exterior of the house for any winter damage, especially cracked steps or walkways.
Clean and store the snowblower.
Wash the windows and clean the screens.
Pack away winter overcoats, boots, etc.
Clean rain gutters and eavestroughs.
Check the condition of outdoor faucets, barbecue, lawnmower, outdoor furniture and outdoor light bulbs.
Check out the local garage sales!!

Sunday May 13
Mother's Day

MOTHER love is the fuel that enables a normal human being to do the impossible.

M. C. Garratty

Monday May 14

FAMILY faces are magic mirrors. Looking at people who belong to us, we see the past, present and future.

Gail Lumet Buckley

I find this to be so true. Many times when I look at my daughters, grandchildren or great-grandchildren I will see something that reminds me of

"Lilac Time"

my own mother. It may be a gesture, a look or a word that will trigger a memory from long ago.

Just recently I was chatting with my great-grandson Justin. As he turned his face to me, the light caught his smile in such a way that he looked just like my late husband when he was Justin's age. For a moment it took my breath away, and then he turned again and the resemblance was gone.

It amazes me to think that some small part of me will be a part of my family generations into the future.

I treasure that thought!

Tuesday May 15

THERE will come a time when you believe everything is finished. That will be the beginning.

Louis L'Amour

Wednesday May 16

ONE of the most difficult decisions that we are ever called upon to make should really be one of the easiest. I am referring to the choice of making organ donations—the gift of life when we or those we love pass away.

Canada, one of the best countries in the world to live, has a very low organ donation rate, among the lowest of the developed countries. Thousands of people across our country are waiting for an organ transplant, and many will die before receiving the necessary organ.

A common misconception is that when we sign a donor or registration card it guarantees that our organs will be used for transplants. In fact, the signature recognizes our willingness to donate, but the ultimate decision regarding donations rests with the family.

Although death is something that most of us are reluctant to talk about, it is wise to let your family know if organ donations are your wish.

It's interesting to know that there is no age barrier for organ donation. Anyone from an infant to the very elderly may be donors.

One such donor was a 104-year-old whose eyes allowed someone to see for the first time. As they say, "Donate your organs. Heaven knows we need them."

Thursday May 17

IN the times of quietness, our hearts should be like trees, lifting their branches to the sky to draw down the strength which they will need to face the storms that will surely come.

Toyohiko Kagawa

Friday May 18

Cause and Effect

Once someone said something
nice about me,
And, all undeserved though
I knew it to be,
I treasured it there
on my heart's deepest self,
Till one day I quite
surprised even myself
By honestly making
an effort to be
That nice thing that
somebody said about me.

Helen Lowrie Marshall

Saturday May 19

IT is another's fault if he be ungrateful, but it is mine if I do not give.

Seneca

Sunday May 20

AND lo I am with you always even to the end of the world.

Matthew 28:20

Monday May 21

BLOSSOM time, for many of us one of the most eagerly awaited times of the year, is very fleeting. However, even brief glimpses of pale pink and white blossoms are welcome respites from the drab grays and browns of winter's end.

There are many blossom festivals all across Canada, but one of the longest-running and best-known celebrations is the Annapolis Valley Apple Blossom Festival.

Since the 1930's, both Canadians and Americans have made the trek to the Kentville-Grand Pré area of Nova Scotia to enjoy the delicately scented blossoms of a million apple trees. Also included in the festival are the Blossom Street Fest barbecued meals, craft shows, sports events and the crowning of Queen Annapolisa, "monarch" of the festival.

If you should have the opportunity to be in this area of the country at this time of year, the Apple Blossom festival is well worth attending.

Tuesday May 22

THE return of good weather means the return, in our family at least, to outdoor cooking. This evening we enjoyed Lamb Burgers with Mint Raitha Sauce.

Lamb Burgers

1 1/2 lb. ground lamb
2 tbsp. tomato ketchup
2 tsp. dried basil
2 tbsp. finely chopped parsley
3 tbsp. finely chopped onions
salt & freshly ground black pepper to taste.

Mix all ingredients together and form 4 one-inch thick patties. Brush with oil. Grill 6 or 7 minutes per side for medium, or 5 minutes per side for medium rare.

Mint Raitha

1/2 cup sour cream or plain yogurt
2 tbsp. mint sauce
1 tbsp. lemon juice
ground black pepper.

Mix all ingredients in a small bowl.

Serve on crusty rolls. Top lamb burgers with mint raitha and a slice of kiwi.

Wednesday May 23

FAILURES are more commonly caused by having made no choice rather than by wrong decisions. *L. Carte*

Thursday May 24
Ascension Day

See the Conqueror mounts in triumph,
See the King in royal state
Riding on the clouds his chariot
To his heavenly palace gate;
Hark! The choirs of angel voices
Joyful alleluias sing,
And the portals high are lifted
To receive their heavenly King.

Bishop Christopher Wordsworth

Friday May 25

MY friend Jake points out that the trouble with jogging is that by the time you realize you are in no condition for it, you've got a long walk to get back home.

Saturday May 26

ALTHOUGH last weekend was the long holiday weekend, when we are usually in Muskoka, we are enjoying the lake this weekend instead. Eleanor had a dreadful case of the flu so we put off opening her cottage until today. As she is still not feeling one hundred per cent, Marg, Bruce and I are doing the few chores necessary to ready the place for summer. Eleanor is most fortunate that her cottage requires very little maintenance. Apart from dusting, vacuuming and window cleaning everything is pretty much ship-shape and ready for use.

This evening we enjoyed sitting by the fire while the muted cries of the loons on the lake came through the windows.

I was reminded of these lines sung so often.

Land of the silver birch
Home of the beaver,
Where still the mighty moose
Wanders at will.
Blue lake and rocky shore
I will return once more
Boom dideada, boom dideada
Boom dideada, boom.

Ontario Camp Song

Sunday May 27

EVERY good gift and every perfect gift is from above, and cometh down from the father of lights, with whom is no variableness, neither shadow of turning.

James 1:17

Monday May 28

THE real proof of courtesy and restraint is to have the same ailment the other person is describing and not mention it.

Tuesday May 29

Sunrise

NOW the king of day plays bo-peep round the world's corner, and every cottage window smiles a golden smile—a very picture of glee. I see the water glistening in the eye. The smothered breathing of awakening day strikes the ear with an undulating motion over hill and dale, pasture and woodland, come they to me, and I am at home in the world.

Henry David Thoreau

Wednesday May 30

AT the risk of sounding old-fashioned, I worry about many of the young women that I see on television today. So frequently they appear to be desperately underweight; some even look skeletal. I worry about these actresses, but of even more concern to me is the example that we are giving to the youngsters who watch television. The stars are often role models for those who watch them. If these role models are wafer thin, it would suggest that young viewers should be likewise. In a day and age when anorexia, bulimia and other eating disorders are on the rise, I feel it is irresponsible that these actresses should be held up as images to be emulated.

Thursday May 31

LIVE each day as if it were your last—one of these days you'll be right.

June

Friday June 1

THERE is not a day goes by that I don't think of my late husband, George, but never more so than on this first day of June, the anniversary of our marriage. Although George passed away too young, the years that we shared still give me wonderful memories. I think he would be so proud to see how our children, grandchildren and great-grandchildren have turned out, and I believe he would have been impressed with the way I have lived my life, as well.

George and I had no secret formula for our successful marriage, but our relationship was built on love, trust and sharing. We shared good times and bad, but through all of them we loved each other.

Today I remember George with love and a grateful heart.

Until we meet again…

Saturday June 2

As my former readers know, ours is a family of chocolate lovers. My grandchildren consider any meal incomplete that does not contain chocolate in some form. My great-grandson Mickey passed along these "Rules of Chocolate" to enjoy.

If you've got melted chocolate all over your hands, you're eating it too slowly.

A nice box of chocolates can provide your daily intake of calories in one place. Isn't that handy?

Chocolate-covered cherries, raisins, orange slices, and strawberries all count as fruit, so you may eat as many as you want.

Diet tip: Eat a chocolate bar before each meal. It will take the edge off your appetite.

If calories are an issue, store your chocolate on top of your fridge. Calories are afraid of heights, and they will jump out of the chocolate to protect themselves.

Eating equal amounts of dark chocolate and white chocolate gives a "balanced diet"... right?

Money talks. Chocolate sings.

Chocolate has many preservatives.

Preservatives make you look younger.

If not for chocolate, there would be no need for control-top pantyhose. An entire garment industry would be devasted.

Put "Eat chocolate" at the top of your list of

things to do today. That way, at least you'll get one thing done.

Sunday June 3

MAKE a joyful noise unto God, all ye lands: Sing forth the honour of His name; make His praise glorious.

Psalm 66:1–2

Monday June 4

MARK Twain's sense of humour has always greatly appealed to me. I particularly enjoyed this story.

Mark Twain happened to be looking across the road at the house opposite to his own. A family whom he had not met had recently moved in. He saw something that caused him to rush across the street and exclaim to the people on the verandah, "My name is Twain. My wife and I fully intend to call upon you and pay our respects, but we have not been able to do so. I beg your pardon for intruding in this abrupt manner but thought I ought to tell you that your house is on fire."

Tuesday June 5

NEVER tell a young person that something cannot be done. God may have been waiting for centuries for somebody ignorant enough of the impossibility to do that thing.

Dr. J. A. Holmes

Wednesday June 6

JUNE is the traditional month for weddings. How well I remember the month of June years ago in our Cape Breton home. Our father was at his busiest during June because he married many of the young people of our area.

My sister, Sarah, and I loved it! We were responsible for decorating the chapel and we spent endless hours picking and arranging the flowers to be placed at the front of the church under the stained-glass windows.

At the appointed time, we would arrive in our prettiest dresses to sit quietly in the back of the church, watching the nervous grooms and radiant brides.

Our young brother, Ben, was a part of the festivities as well. He was the official bell-ringer at the end of the ceremony. My, how those bells would peel as Ben put all of his energy into pulling the rope!

These are treasured memories from my months of June.

Thursday June 7

ANY wife can help keep springtime in her husband's eyes by keeping a fresh flower in her hair. Any husband can keep springtime in his wife's heart by supplying the flower.

Oren Arnold

Friday June 8

THE service we render for others is really the rent we pay for our room on the earth.

Wilfred Grenfell

Saturday June 9

HOW quickly my birthday seems to have come again. This year the whole family joined together and we went to a strawberry-picking farm. Although I no longer pick the berries, I do enjoy walking through the gift shop.

When we arrived home, everyone set about preparing the berries for jam. It was truly a day where "many hands make light work," and by evening, we had dozens of jars of jam to store or to share with friends.

We also enjoyed a wonderful strawberry short-cake/birthday cake and I couldn't help remarking that, if one must acknowledge another birthday, having it with the family is a delightful way to do it.

Sunday June 10

BEHOLD, I stand at the door and knock: if any man hear my voice, and open the door, I will come in to him, and will sup with him and he with me.

Revelations 3: 20

Monday June 11

I DRAW comfort from these words of William Lyon Phelps.

"I know of no greater fallacy nor one more widely believed, than the statement that youth is the happiest time of life. As we advance in years, we grow happier if we live intelligently. Difficulties and responsibilities strengthen and enrich the mind. To live abundantly is like climbing a mountain or a tower. To say that youth is happier than maturity is like saying the view from the bottom of the tower is better than the view from the top. As we ascend, the range of our view widens. The horizon is pushed further away.

Finally we reach the summit, and it is as if we had the world at our feet."

Tuesday June 12

MY friend Peggy, who runs a bed and breakfast inn in the Cotswold area of England, often sends along her household tips for me. As someone who has spent many years preparing meals for her guests, Peggy's hints are usually "tried and true." I offer several of her ideas to you today.

Use a meat baster to squeeze pancake batter on to the hot griddle. It gives perfectly shaped pancakes every time.

To easily remove burned-on food from a skillet, add a drop or two of dish soap and enough water to cover the bottom of the pan. Bring to a boil for several minutes. Your pan will now clean easily.

To soften brown sugar that has hardened, add a slice of apple.

Potatoes will take food stains off your fingers. Slice and rub raw potato on the stains, and rinse with water.

If you've accidentally over salted a dish while cooking, add a peeled potato while still cooking—it will absorb excess salt.

Wednesday June 13

MONTHS and days I've wasted
Doing some useless thing...
How few the hours that have been well spent
Viewing the flowers of Spring.

Fujiwara Okizawa

Thursday June 14

I RECENTLY heard a neighbour moaning, "Oh I don't think I can learn to use a computer. I'm too old."

Consider the accomplishments of these people, all over the age of 75.

At age 80, Grandma Moses was still painting.

Winston Churchill wrote his four-volume "A History of the English-speaking Peoples" at 82.

Pablo Picasso was drawing and engraving at 92.

Arthur Rubenstein performed one of his greatest piano recitals at age 89.

Michelangelo designed the church of Santa Maria degli Angeli when he was 86.

George Bernard Shaw was still writing plays at 93.

John Glenn flew in the space shuttle when he was a "youngster" of 77.

You are never too old to try something new!

Friday June 15

WE'VE got this gift of love, but love is like a precious plant. You can't just accept it and leave it in the cupboard, or just think it's going to get on by itself.

You've got to keep watering it. You've got to really look after and nurture it.

John Lennon

"June Bride"

C Black

Saturday June 16

FREDERIC Amiel offers wise advice:

Learn to limit yourself, to content yourself with some definite thing and some definite work;

Dare to be what you are, and learn to resign with a good grace all that you are not, and to believe in your own individuality.

Sunday June 17
Father's Day

A NATIVE American of the Seneca Nation, Yehwenode spoke of the wisdom of his grandfather.

"My grandfather, Red Jacket, offered simple teachings. For example, each person should ask himself or herself four important questions that can serve as a guide to living.

Am I happy in what I am doing?

Is what I am doing going to add to the confusion in the world?

What am I doing to bring about peace and contentment?

How will I be remembered when I am gone?"

Monday June 18

AS baseball season rolls along, my friend Jake enjoys telling interesting but little-known stories from America's favourite pastime.

There is, in the National Baseball Hall of Fame, a photo of a man who never played a single inning of professional baseball. How his picture came to be there is a story in itself.

When the Hall of Fame was being renovated in 1994, workers moved a case that highlighted baseball during the Second World War. Underneath the case they found a picture of a man holding a bat, wearing a shirt that said "Sinclair" on the front. Attached to the photo was a handwritten note that read, "You were never too tired to play catch. On your days off you helped build the little league field. You always came to watch me play. You were a Hall of Fame Dad. I wish I could share this moment with you. Your son, Pat."

It took a lot of investigation, but it turns out that the picture was of "Big Joe" O'Donnell. His son, Pat, took the picture with him when he visited the Hall of Fame in 1988, for the first time. When no one was looking, he slipped the picture under the cabinet, telling no one but his close family what he had done.

When the renovations were completed, Ted Spencer, curator of exhibits, slipped the photo under another exhibit with a note to the future curators asking that the picture be left as a "gift to every parent who has taken the time to play baseball with their children."

Tuesday June 19

CHINESE-CANADIANS have a celebration near the fifth day of the fifth moon on the Chinese calendar.

The Dragon Boat Festival honours an ancient Chinese poet and statesman, Qu Yuan, who drowned himself in protest against political corruption and injustice. According to legend, as the townspeople tried to rescue him, they beat their drums and splashed their oars to frighten away the fish and the water dragons. To keep the fish from eating Qu Yuan's body, the fishermen threw a dumpling made from meat and rice and wrapped in bamboo leaves into the river.

Today, festival activities recall the legendary event.

To symbolize attempts to rescue Qu Yuan, participants race elaborately decorated, narrow dragon boats. These boats measure 12 metres in length and have ornately carved and painted dragon heads and tails. Each boat carries 22 paddlers.

The Canadian International Dragon Boat Festival, held in Vancouver, is a truly unique event. At the Plaza of Nations, on the shores of False Creek, there is a three day presentation of the performing and visual arts. The performers come from the professional and semi-professional arts community of Canada, along with special guests from Pacific Rim countries. Add a culinary festival, the dragon boat races, and you have an event for all to enjoy.

Wednesday June 20

THE difference between a prejudice and a conviction is that you can explain a conviction without getting mad.

Thursday June 21

SUMMER begins sometime today and I, for one, welcome it with open arms. The older I get, the more I seem to enjoy the long, hot days that come with this season.

We all wish summer would never end, that our hair would never gray and that our bodies would never tire.

C. Swayze

Friday June 22

WHEN you finally go back to your old home town, you find it wasn't the old home town that you missed, but your childhood.

Sam Ewing

Saturday June 23

BOXING, as a sport, has never interested me, nor was it of interest to my husband, George. I admit, however, that I have been touched by Mohammed Ali, a former Olympic boxer and world champion, who, despite ravages of Parkinson's syndrome, carries great influence with many young people today. Who can forget the sight of this once strong athlete as he held the torch high to light the Olympic flame for the 1996 Olympic Games in Atlanta?

Adults and children alike still look up to Ali and he continues to give many young people encouraging advice.

Stay in college, get the knowledge;

Stay there 'til you're through.

If they can make penicillin out of moldy bread,

They can sure make something out of you!

Sunday June 24

Summer suns are glowing

Over land and sea,

"Summer Daydream"

C Block

Happy light is flowing,
Beautiful and free,
Everything rejoices
In the mellow rays,
All earth's thousand voices,
Swell the psalm of praise.

Bishop W. Walsham Howe

Monday June 25

MY friend Jake enjoys fishing very much. This poem is especially for him.

Time To Go Fishing

Time to go fishing: to sit in a boat
Or wade in a stream,
To wear an old hat, an old shirt, and no coat
And maybe dream.

Time to go fishing; away from the town,
It's stress and it's strain
To depart from the shore, every burden put down,
And be humble again.

Time to go fishing; pride's vestments to leave
On a hook or a shelf,
To drop all the shams that go to deceive
And just be yourself.

Time to go fishing; no matter the spot
Or sunshine or rain,
And return to the town whether lucky or not,
To brave life again.

Edgar A. Guest

Tuesday June 26

IT'S what we learn after we think we know it all that counts.

Abe Martin

Wednesday June 27

TOMORROW is often the busiest day of the year.

Spanish Proverb

Thursday June 28

WHEN I was a child, any pennies that I received were almost invariably spent on licorice. To this day I still enjoy soft black licorice candy and some of the best licorice I ever ate was during my visit to New Zealand. I found it interesting to learn that people have been enjoying licorice, in one form or another, for centuries. Archeologists discovered stone tablets near Baghdad describing how it was used to treat their Royal masters seven centuries before Christ.

Licorice root was found in the tomb of Tutankhamen. In the Middle Ages, it became popular as a sweet medicine. It has been used as a beautifying agent, a remedy for coughs and as a treatment for hair loss.

I just love to eat it!

Friday June 29

LIFE is a lot like a vacation. We're so fixed on the idea of where we're going that we don't appreciate the ride along the way.

Saturday June 30

MY good friends Will and Muriel recently celebrated their 50th wedding anniversary. Their family provided a wonderful gift for them that they will treasure for years. Their children asked that friends and family members write letters or cards recalling a special memory shared with Will and Muriel. The children put all of the cards and letters in an album which they presented to their parents at the anniversary party.

Will and Muriel were delighted! Many of the letters came from friends they hadn't heard from in years, and the memories shared are real treasures.

Muriel spoke for them both when she said,

"This is a book we will enjoy over and over for the rest of our lives. You couldn't have given us a finer gift than these beautiful memories.

Thank you all!"

July

Sunday July 1

ALMIGHTY God, we thank you for making the fruitful earth produce what is needed for life. Bless those who work in the field, give us favourable weather and grant that all might share the fruits of the earth, rejoicing in your goodness, through Jesus Christ our Lord. Amen.

Monday July 2

YESTERDAY was the day for each and every one of us to celebrate the love of our country. On this day, in 1867, the British North America Act proclaimed "the Provinces...into one Dominion" under the name of Canada. The B.N.A. Act was renamed the Constitution Act and was repatriated in September of 1981.

Celebrations across the country are always many and varied on this day. Our family enjoyed a marvellous fireworks display in our local park. No matter how we celebrate, we are extremely lucky to be living in what I believe is the best country in the world, Canada!

Tuesday July 3

> Oh, the summer night
> Has a smile of light
> And she sits on a sapphire throne.

> *From "The Nights"*
> *B. W. Procter*

Wednesday July 4

TODAY is the day that our wonderful neighbours to the south celebrate their "Glorious Fourth." Americans from north to south and east to west will celebrate the birthdate of their country with much boisterous enthusiasm and flag waving.

Along with the American flag, one of the most well known symbols of the United States of America is the Liberty Bell. Here are just a few little known facts about the Liberty Bell.

The Liberty Bell was cast by Thomas Lester of Whitechapel, London, England. It arrived in Philadelphia in August, 1752. It was first used in the State House at Philadelphia on August 27, 1752. It took its first journey from Philadelphia to Allentown in September, 1775 to escape capture by the British. It proclaimed the birth of a new nation on July 8, 1776.

It was returned to Allentown on June 27, 1778. It cracked in tolling the death of John Marshall on July 8, 1835.

Thursday July 5

YOU are the bows from which your children as living arrows are sent forth. The Archer sees the mark upon the path of the infinite, and He bends you with His might that His arrows may go swift and far.

Let your bending in the Archer's hand be for gladness;

For even as He loves that arrow that flies, so He loves also the bow that is stable.

Kahlil Gibran

Friday July 6

OLD age is like a plane flying through a storm. Once you are aboard, there is nothing you can do.

Saturday July 7

ERNEST Hemingway once received a sarcastic note implying that the writer was overpaid.

"I know that your price is now a dollar a word. I am enclosing one dollar with the request that you send me a sample."

Hemingway kept the dollar and replied simply, "Thanks."

Sunday July 8

THIS prayer comes from Abdu'l-Baha, of the Baha'i faith.

Moreover, a soul of excellent deeds and good manners will undoubtedly advance from whatever horizon he beholdeth the lights radiating. Herein lies the difference: by faith is meant, first, conscious knowledge, and second, the practice of good deeds.

Monday July 9

TODAY, in our family, we have a double celebration. It is Phyllis and Bill's wedding anniversary, and as well, it is the birthday of the twins, Justin and Jenny. My, how the years have flown. It seems like only yesterday that we were looking at two very tiny babies in incubators and here they are today, young adults.

I couldn't help but think how proud my husband, George, would be today. Family was so important to him, and ours seems to have turned out so well.

"Every family has its own history, its own heartbeat…a family is where life begins and love happens."

Tuesday July 10

MY friend Jake offered these ideas on "how to tell if you are growing old." Although I found them to be humorous, they are almost too close to the truth.

Everything hurts and what doesn't hurt, doesn't work.
You get winded playing chess.
Your children are starting to look middle aged.
You turn out the lights for economic rather than romantic reasons.

Your knees buckle, but your belt won't.

You burn the midnight oil until 9 p.m.

The little gray-haired lady you help across the street is your wife.

You get your exercise acting as a pallbearer for your friends who exercise.

Your pacemaker sets off the check-out alarms in the mall.

You have too much room in your house and not nearly enough in your medicine cabinet.

Wednesday July 11

TODAY, Lila and I were reminiscing about our childhoods, and Lila was very interested in the names of some of my childhood friends. For those of you not familiar with the history of the settlement of Cape Breton, I hope this explanation will interest you as it did Lila.

In the 18th century, after an unsuccessful attempt to put "Bonnie" Prince Charlie on the throne of England, thousands of highlanders fled to Canada. About 25,000 Scottish immigrants, representing the 14 major Scottish clans, settled on Cape Breton Island. Most families chose from among five Christian names for male children. For example, 177 of the 210 McDonalds in Antigonish county, were named John, Donald, Angus, Allan or Alex.

The solution to the identity problem was to

add a nickname to link each person to a particular place or incident. For example, of the Angus McDonalds, there was Angus Boots (his father owned a shoe store), Six-Foot Angus (the tallest of the bunch), Angus Schoolhouse (his home was closest to school) and Angus the Nun (he was a convent janitor).

I have a friend to this day who is John the Post (a mailman). It is just another interesting part of our Canadian heritage.

Thursday July 12

THIS is a wonderful time of the year for outdoor barbecues and one of the most often chosen meats to barbecue is chicken. I hope that you enjoy this recipe for Spiced Grilled Chicken with special BBQ sauce.

1/4 cup packed dark brown sugar
2 tbsp. paprika
2 tbsp. garlic powder
1 tbsp. chili powder
1 tbsp. ground cumin
1 tsp. pepper
salt to taste
1/8 tsp. cayenne pepper
8 pounds chicken pieces (about 24 pieces)
1 cup ketchup
3/4 cup cider vinegar

6 tbsp. dark molasses

2 tbsp. Worcestershire sauce.

Combine first 8 ingredients and mix well. Rub over all sides of the chicken to coat well. Cover and refrigerate at least two hours (or overnight).

Light only one side of grill.

Cook chicken over unlit side of grill—in batches if necessary—until no longer pink at the bone (about 15-20 minutes per side).

In a bowl, combine ketchup, vinegar, molasses and Worcestershire sauce. Serve with the chicken. Makes 12 servings.

Friday July 13

TACT is the rare ability to keep silent while two friends are arguing, and you know both of them are wrong.

Hugh Allen

Saturday July 14

MY grandson Marshall really enjoys his Saturday morning golf games with his dad. Marshall was particularly enthusiastic when he came in today.

"Gran, I sunk a "Payne Stewart, U.S. Open" putt this morning. It was beautiful."

Marshall was referring, of course, to the 15-

foot putt that golfing great Payne Stewart sunk at the Pinehurst Golf Club in June 1999 to win the U.S. Open golf title.

Payne Stewart was an exceptional golfer, husband and father. Known for his fashion style on the course—he chose to wear plus fours (knickers), argyle socks and caps in deference to the early players of the game—he was a standout.

According to fellow golfers, he was one of the "nice guys" on the tour, often giving his time to coach younger players or to lend his presence at charitable functions.

Stewart was killed in a plane crash in 1999, but the sight of his wide stance—fist in the air with joy at winning the Open—will long be remembered, especially by all who love the game of golf.

Sunday July 15

LET the words of my mouth and the meditation of my heart, be always acceptable in thy sight, O Lord, my strength and my redeemer.

Psalm 19:14

Monday July 16

TWO years ago today the world lost yet another member of the Kennedy family. John Kennedy (son of former president Kennedy), his wife, Caroline, and her sister

Lauren perished in the crash of a single-engine plane in the ocean off Martha's Vineyard. As his uncle, Ted Kennedy, would say at the memorial service, "Like his father, he had every gift but length of years."

The Kennedys are of Irish background, and I remembered this old Irish blessing today:

May the earth be soft under you when you rest upon it, tired at the end of a day, and may it rest easy over you when, at last, you lie under it.

May it rest so lightly over you that your soul may be off from under it quickly, and up and off, and on its way to God.

And now may the Lord bless you and bless you kindly.

Tuesday July 17

AS baseball season moves along, our neighbour Roger offers these observations from some bygone "experts" of the game.

"We plan absentee ownership. I'll stick to building ships."
—George Steinbrenner, shipping executive, speculating on his future role as owner of the New York Yankees, in 1973.

"Just so-so in centre field."
—*New York Daily News*, assessing rookie Willie Mays, in 1951.

"I don't like the way he stands at the plate...I don't believe this kid will ever hit…"
—Bill Cunningham, Boston sports writer, appraising Red Sox rookie Ted Williams, in 1938.

"Ruth made a big mistake when he gave up pitching. Working once a week, he might last a long time and become a great star."
—Tris Speaker, commenting on Babe Ruth's plan to change from pitcher to an outfielder, in 1921.

Wednesday July 18

THE reason why birds fly and we can't is simply that they have perfect faith, for to have perfect faith is to have wings.

James M. Barrie

Thursday July 19

Kind hearts are the gardens,
Kind thoughts are the roots,
Kind words are the flowers,
Kind deeds are the fruits.

Take care of the gardens,
And keep them from weeds.
Fill, fill them with flowers,
Kind words and kind deeds.

Henry Wadsworth Longfellow

Friday July 20

SEVERAL of my friends who have been widowed for many years were discussing the difficulty of establishing a new relationship with a gentleman.

Edith made us all laugh when she said, "You know, finding a husband at our ages is like finding a parking place. You have to be right behind someone who is moving out."

Saturday July 21

DURING the summer vacation from school, many parents and grandparents are looking for activities for children that are fun and entertaining—but also inexpensive.

Friends and I came up with a number of ideas that might be enjoyed by young and old alike.

Airplanes are fascinating. Pack a picnic lunch and take it to your local airport to watch planes take off and land. We used to make up stories about each plane's destination, with a chocolate bar going to the best storyteller.

Let the children clean out their rooms and hold a garage sale with the unwanted items. They get to keep the money to spend themselves, or they may choose to pool their funds to pay for an outing to a movie or another entertainment of their choice.

Two cups of dishwashing liquid mixed with 6 cups of water and 3/4 cup of light corn syrup or glycerin make great bubble-blowing liquid. You can make giant bubbles by using string to tie four drinking straws into a square for dipping. Any remaining liquid can be stored in a jar.

Sheets, blankets and chairs make great "tents," or "forts" indoors or out. Children will spend hours making rooms in these tents, and it is a great place to read a book.

A little imagination can provide many hours of inexpensive pleasure.

Sunday July 22

Sleep, my love, and peace attend thee,
All through the night;
Guardian angels God will lend thee,
All through the night;
Soft the drowsy hours are creeping
Hill and dale in slumber steeping,
Love alone his watch is keeping—
All through the night.

Anonymous

Monday July 23

TODAY is Marg and Bill's wedding anniversary. There is a beautiful Apache blessing that is being read more and more often at wedding ceremonies of all denominations.

I find it very moving and I offer it to Bill and Marg on this special day.

Now you will feel no rain,
For each of you will be shelter to each other.
Now you will feel no cold,
For each of you will be warmth to each other.
Now you are two bodies,
But there is only one life before you.
Go now to your dwelling place,
To enter into the days of your togetherness.
And may your days be good, and long upon the
earth.

Tuesday July 24

CHEERFULNESS and contentment are great beautifiers and are famous preservers of youthful looks.

Charles Dickens

Wednesday July 25

THERE is a serene and settled majesty to woodland scenery that enters into the soul and delights and elevates it, and fills it with noble inclinations.

Washington Irving

Thursday July 26

NATURE is painting for us, day after day, pictures of infinite beauty, if only we have eyes to see.

John Ruskin

Friday July 27

HERE is a young salesman who'll go places.

A customer asked for help, saying, "I want to buy a stick."

"Certainly, sir," was the reply. "Shaving, walking, candle or lip?"

Saturday July 28

MANY older people are unimpressed with the youth of the day. I would like to tell you a story that I think could change those opinions.

One of the lawn and garden centres in our area generously donated a large section of their farm to our local nursing home residents. The idea was that the residents would have a garden to call their own, to be planted with flowers of their choosing. Because spring and summer are the two busiest months of the year, the staff at the centre wouldn't be able to keep the gardens weeded and watered. That was where the students at the local high school stepped in. When the appeal for volunteers went out, back in May, numerous students stepped up to help. With the assistance of several teachers, a schedule was drawn up for weeding and watering through all of the summer months.

I recently took Lila out to see the garden, and we were both very impressed with the work that has been done by the young people. Several students were there working, and they were pleased to show us their handiwork. The garden was weed free and obviously well cared for. As well, a number of comfortable chairs and benches had been added so that visitors may sit and enjoy the beauty of the gardens.

These young people give us reason to be proud.

Sunday July 29

BE perfect, be of good comfort, be of one mind, live in peace; and the God of love and peace shall be with you.

II Corinthians 13:11

Monday July 30

> Raised are the dripping oars,
> Silent the boat! The lake
> Lovely and soft as a dream,
> Swims in the sheen of the moon.

Matthew Arnold

Tuesday July 31

GRANDPARENTS should be one of a child's most valuable resources. They should be gentle teachers of the way life was and the way it should be.

John Rosemond

August

Wednesday August 1

Midsummer Pause

There is a moment in midsummer when the
earth pauses between flower and fruit; the hay
is cut,
the oats ripen on pasture knolls,
dew pearly everlasting
lifts its small fountains of silver and gold.

The skies are blue, the hills rest all day
like men at noon under a shady tree.
The leaves have turned dark green, they hoard
their strength, no strong wind harms them.
Boys swim under the big elm by the crick.
Locusts drone in the trees; the swallows
gather on wires, and starlings in flocks
wheel over the meadows like curving hands.

Fred Lape

Thursday August 2

AS the traveller who has once been from
home is wiser than he who has never left his

own doorstep, so a knowledge of one other culture should sharpen our ability to appreciate more lovingly our own.

Margaret Mead

Friday August 3

AROUND this time of year here in Canada, students are making a decision about which university they will attend in the fall. Although the larger universities may offer a wider selection of courses, some young people prefer the more personal connections offered by a small college or university. Whether attending a large or a small school, no student wants to be just a number.

One young man in the United States found that he was just a number. When he received his acceptance from Arizona State University, his parents also received a letter of congratulations from the parents' association. The letter read, "Congratulations on 987-65-4321's admission to Arizona State University. We are fully prepared to assist 987-65-4321 in making a successful transition to college."

His father wrote back, "Thank you for offering our son, 987-65-4321, or as we affectionately refer to him—987—a position in your university. His mother, 123-45-6MOM, and I are very proud. From 123-45-6DAD."

In spite of receiving an apology for the

computer error in the acceptance letter, the young man accepted a position at a different university.

Saturday August 4

A CLEAR conscience is a soft pillow.

Sunday August 5

What a friend we have in Jesus,
All our sins and grief to bear!
What a privilege to carry
Everything to God in prayer!

O, what peace we often forfeit,
O, what needless pain we bear
All because we do not carry
Everything to God in prayer.

Joseph Scriven

Many of you are probably very familiar with this lovely hymn. You may not, however, know much of its author, Joseph Medlicott Scriven, who now rests in a small pioneer cemetery near Bailieboro, Ontario, not far from Rice Lake.

Born in Seapatrick, County Down, Ireland, he attended Trinity College in Dublin, where he graduated in theology.

"Summer
Roses"

He became engaged to a young lady, but on the eve of the wedding, while horseback riding, she jumped a fence, landed in a ditch and drowned before Scriven could rescue her.

Early in 1845, the heartbroken Scriven made his first visit to Canada. Still unsettled, he returned to Ireland, where he began his famous hymn.

Returning to Canada once again, he moved into the Port Hope area where he worked as a tutor for the children of Captain R. L. Pengally. The family were members of the Plymouth Brethren, an offshoot of the Anglican Church, and their puritan morality so appealed to Scriven that he became one of the brethren's most famous preachers.

He met and fell in love with Mrs. Pengally's niece, Catherine Roche. Her conversion to the Brethren faith required total immersion during baptism. In April, Catherine was immersed in the icy waters of Rice Lake. Tragedy struck again when, before wedding vows could be exchanged, she developed pneumonia and died.

Scriven spent the rest of his life in self-deprivation and service to God. His hymn, which he completed while living in Port Hope, was finally printed in *Gospel Hymns*, and Scriven was recognized as the author (there having been an incorrect attribution to Rev. Horatius Bonar).

Scriven died in 1886 and was buried in the Pengally cemetery near his beloved Catherine.

Although he had a lifetime of personal calamities, he has left the world a beautiful hymn to cherish.

Monday August 6

THIS is the holiday that we know as the Civic Holiday, here in Ontario. Honouring our first lieutenant-governor of the province, John Graves Simcoe, it is also known as Simcoe Day. It is a wonderful summer's day for all to enjoy!

Tuesday August 7

THE dictionary defines an optimist as "one who takes the most hopeful view of matters." I am an optimist and find that most people I know are likewise. My good friend Muriel gave me this amusing list of "optimists."

An optimist is:
A man who goes on a fishing trip carrying a camera and a frying pan.

A driver who thinks that the empty space beside the road won't have a fire hydrant next to it.

A person who plans what to do with the money left over after the taxes.

A person who starts to do up their jacket when the speaker says, "And in conclusion…."

Wednesday August 8

I LIKE the motto of the New Hampton Preparatory School of New Hampton, New Hampshire.

In a world that expects you to fit in, we teach you to stand out.

Thursday August 9

MY sons-in-law Bruce and John played a round of golf this evening. John offered this little poem as the answer to my query, "How was your game?" My thanks to the unknown author.

Although my drives are not too far,
And chip shots not spectacular,
And even when I reach the green,
My putting eye is not too keen,
But still I love the game a lot,
I'm happy making every shot;
The only part that I abhor
Is when I total up the score.

Friday August 10

THIS evening Marg and Bruce will be kind enough to drive me north to my dear friend Eleanor's cottage in Muskoka. For as many years as I can remember, I have spent a week or more with Eleanor in this most beautiful area of Ontario. No matter how often I visit, there is a beauty and peace that restores my soul as little else does.

I look forward to the beauty of Muskoka, but even more, I look forward to spending days in the companionship of a dear and loved friend.

"A friend may well be reckoned the masterpiece of nature."

Ralph Waldo Emerson

Saturday August 11

ELEANOR, Marg, Bruce and I took a lovely cruise around the lake today. It was a glorious day to be out on the water and we enjoyed it immensely. We made several stops along the way but I most enjoyed our visit to the small Indian Village in Port Carling. While there, I purchased dream catchers for my great-grandchildren Bethany and Michael.

For many generations, many Native Americans of North America, have held the hoop in the highest esteem because it symbolizes unity and strength.

The dream catcher is a traditional symbol that has been handed down through the generations. The hoop is made from a willow branch, and decorated with a web of string, feathers and other bits of everyday life. It is believed to have the power to catch all of its owner's dreams, filtering the bad and letting only the good dreams pass through.

The following was written on the card attached to my dream catcher.

The native people believe that the night air is filled with dreams, good and bad. The dream catcher, when hung in your place of rest, swinging freely with the air, catches the dreams as they flow by. The good dreams know the way, slipping through the outer holes and sliding down the feathers so gently that they land almost unnoticed on the sleeper. The bad dreams, not knowing the way, become tangled in the web and perish with the first light of day.

Sunday August 12

Holy Father, cheer our way
With thy love's perpetual ray;
Grant us every closing day
Light at evening time.

Holy Saviour, calm our fears
When earth's brightness disappears;

Grant us in our latter years
Light at evening time.

Rev. R. H. Robinson

Monday August 13

SUMMERTIME in Canada is the time when families enjoy the country's many parks, with their majestic forests and pristine lakes and rivers. In recent years, camping has realized a renewed popularity, particularly among families with young children. Camping offers a less expensive way to have a vacation, and many of our parks provide outstanding facilities for campers of all ages.

I am quick to admit that at my advanced age, camping holds little appeal. However, I enjoy listening to the stories that my grandchildren and great-grandchildren tell of adventures in their tents.

Tuesday August 14

WHENEVER Eleanor and I are together our conversation turns to family. We often speak about what we hope our families will remember of us. Eleanor pulled out a column from an old newspaper that had yellowed with age. We both enjoyed its enduring wisdom.

"My children are grown now and I have wonderful grandchildren. I love them all, but please God, let me remember that I have lived, loved and enjoyed this life. Do not let me take away from their enjoyment by complaining about every ache and pain. I have earned them all.

"Please keep me from mentioning my swollen joints, stiff knees, poor eyesight and anything else that isn't as good as it once was. Let me remember that I have enjoyed a full and wonderful life, and have been blessed in so many ways. Now is not the time for me to begin complaining.

"Please let my mouth be closed while my ears are open to hear the fun they are having. Let me remember that I am still setting an example for them and if I keep quiet, they will forever think that I never had a single ache or pain in my life and that I miraculously escaped the ills of old age.

"They will, in later years, remember me with pleasure and say, 'I wish I had her genes. She never had anything wrong with her!'

"That, dear Lord, will be the best legacy I can leave them."

Wednesday August 15

HUMANKIND has not woven the web of life. We are but one thread within it. Whatever we do to the web, we do to ourselves.

All things are bound together.
All things connect.

Chief Seattle

Thursday August 16

Yesterday was history,
Tomorrow is a mystery...
Today is a gift.
That's why we call it the present.

Friday August 17

SILENTLY, one by one, in the infinite meadows of heaven, blossomed the lovely stars, the forget-me-nots of angels.

Henry Wadsworth Longfellow

As Eleanor and I sat on the dock this evening, we watched the stars come out, one by one, until the sky was a myriad of tiny white lights. There was a soft breeze blowing through the trees and two loons called back and forth in the deepening darkness of the night.

It is a memory that will pull me back here in the dark and cold of winter.

Saturday August 18

IT seems as if there is always something for the young people to do here in Muskoka. The children next door had a wonderful day on the water. The four youngsters, aged six to 14, had a full day of waterskiing and wakeboarding lessons from Muskoka Pro Ski, an enterprising group run by Jeff Barnes. A team of instructors comes to your cottage with a beautiful, new boat, and the newest and best skis and boards, ready to help you learn the fundamentals of waterskiing or wakeboarding. If you are already proficient, the instructors take you to more advanced levels.

The nicest part is that Muskoka Pro Ski comes right to your dock to spend several hours or all day with you.

Today, Jeff and Jamie, two instructors, taught the children several new skills. The biggest cheer, however, was reserved for six-year-old Mark, who made a complete circuit on the skis on only his second attempt.

Eleanor and I could barely take our eyes off the children as we marvelled at their incredible progress.

Ah, the joys of youth!

Sunday August 19

A MERRY heart doeth good like a medicine.

Proverbs 17: 22

Monday August 20

THIS truth I find implicit in the sunset—while we, from one point of view, are departing from the light of our life, we are at the same time, approaching it from another angle, the resurgent angle of daybreak.

Oscar Ostlund

Tuesday August 21

ON our walk this morning, I was surprised to see a number of trees with leaves already beginning to turn colour. One maple, in particular was a bright scarlet colour, a standout in the green woods.

If the leaves are already changing, can fall be far behind?

Wednesday August 22

IN summer, many of our local radio announcers are aware of the large number of American visitors to the area.

Eleanor and I both chuckled this morning as

the weather reporter announced, "It's currently 21 degrees Celsius—that's 70 degrees on the understandable scale."

Thursday August 23

I CAN see how it might be possible for a man to look down upon the earth and be an atheist, but I can not conceive how he could look up into the heavens and say there is no God.

Abraham Lincoln

Friday August 24

NEVER fear shadows. They simply mean there's a light shining somewhere nearby.

Saturday August 25

WHEN saving for old age, be sure to put away some pleasant memories.

Sunday August 26

IF I take the wings of the morning, and dwell in the uttermost parts of the sea; Even there shall thy hand lead me, and thy right hand shall hold me.

Psalm 139: 9–10

Monday August 27

IT'S hard to believe that my holidays with Eleanor are over. It seems that time spent in the company of dear friends passes so quickly. Many people much more eloquent than I have written of friendship. I offer several of these thoughts today.

As gold more splendid from the fire appears,
Thus friendship brightens by the length of years.

Thomas Carlyle

None is so rich that he or she can afford to lose a friend.

M. McCann

One of the most beautiful qualities of true friendship is to understand and to be understood.

Seneca

Tuesday August 28

Blue to the north is a sky so clear
It means the corner of the year
Has been turned, from now on all
Leaves and men face to the fall.

R. P. T. Coffin

Wednesday August 29

THE summer vacation from school is rapidly drawing to a close. Although most parents are probably breathing a large sigh of relief, I for one will really miss the children when they return to classes. I enjoy having our young neighbours pop in for a chat. Talking with these youngsters is a way for me to keep up with the thoughts and interests of today's young people. In a way, it's a chance for me to stay current in my old age. My loss is the teachers' gain.

Thursday August 30

If I should win, let it be by the code
With my faith and my honour held high;
But if I should lose, let me stand by the road
And cheer as the winners go by.

Author unknown

Friday August 31

THE essence of courage is not that your heart should not quake, but that nobody else should know that it does.

E. F. Benson

September

Saturday September 1

Summer's End

When roses red, their petals shed
Beside the garden wall,
The summer's drawing to a close,
And it's nigh approaching fall.

The orchards' trees will turn their leaves
To radiant hues of brown
And from the heavy-laden boughs
The fruit comes tumbling down.

The feathered friends have left their nests,
Prepared to wend their ways
Down south, a haven warm to find,
To spend their winter days.

The forest creatures scurry round
In search of food and shelter,
A cozy nook in which to bide
The cold and blustery weather.

Margaret Jewell

It's hard to imagine that September is here
again and our summer is nearly over. This is our
last long weekend before autumn. Enjoy it!

Sunday September 2

> Praise his blessed name forever!
> There is naught that can compare,
> To the glories of a contact
> With the Lord our God through prayer.

Anonymous

Monday September 3
Labour Day

THE Labour Day holiday falls on the first Monday in September. More than 100 years ago, workers in Canada, particularly new immigrants, worked in unspeakable conditions for next to no pay. When the trade unions were finally given recognition in 1872, the leaders and union members wanted their political strength and solidarity to be remembered. In 1984, after petitions to the government were finally heeded, Labour Day was declared, by an act of parliament, a national holiday.

I believe these words give us the true meaning of Labour Day:

No man is born into the world whose work is not born with him; there is always work, and tools to work withal, for those who will: and blessed are the horny hands of toil!

James Russell Lowel

Tuesday September 4

IN most provinces across the country, this is the first day of school.

Although many children grumble about returning to class, their protests are often just for show. Most youngsters look forward to seeing their classmates and renewing friendships that are often on hold because of summer vacation.

Most children, whether they admit it or not, thrive on the structure and organization that school brings to their lives. Though everyone needs vacation time, the return to school is welcomed.

Wednesday September 5

I THINK that many parents may find some useful advice in these suggestions.

Frame anything that your child brings home on the first day of school.

Get to know your child's teacher.
Teach your children respect for their teachers and the other people who work hard to make their school an enjoyable place to be.

Children need to be accountable. Let them accept the consequences of their actions.

Thursday September 6

IN the United States, there is a special day set aside in September called "Grandparents' Day". This day was established in 1978 by then president Jimmy Carter, not as a day of gift giving, but of participation in grandchildren's school classes or special assembly programs.

Although this is not an official holiday in Canada, I like to commemorate the day with a visit or a chat on the telephone with each of my grandchildren.

Grandchildren truly are God's reward for growing old.

Friday September 7

ONE looks back with appreciation to the brilliant teachers, but with gratitude to those who touched our human feelings. The curriculum is so much necessary raw material, but warmth is the vital element for the growing plant and for the soul of the child.

Carl Jung

Saturday September 8

WHEN someone tells you something defies description, you may be pretty sure he's going to have a go at it anyway.

"Autumn Leaves"

Sunday September 9

O Lord, transform our selfish hearts
And help us always see
That gentleness and courtesy
Describe how we should be.

Canon R. Hill

Monday September 10

MANY seniors take advantage of the travel bargains offered at this time of year. There are numerous two- and three-day trips to see the wonderful autumn colours. Marg's friend, Joyce who is a travel agent, offered some sound advice for travellers staying in hotels.

Never leave your luggage or handbag unattended in a public area—even for a minute.

Guest room doors should have an automatic closure. Nonetheless, check your door when entering or exiting to be sure that it has closed securely and is locked.

Never leave your door unlocked or ajar when going for ice.

Make sure that you review the emergency exit plans found on the inside of your room door, near the elevators or in the hallways. Be sure you know more than one escape route.

Use your common sense—and enjoy your trip.

Tuesday September 11

A S you know, education has been in a state of flux for the last few years. I really enjoyed reading "Track-Meet Guidelines," by Sue Amos, a Halton Board of Education consultant, who has a bit of fun with some of the changes.

As you are aware, we are in a time of change. Therefore, it should be no surprise to see modifications to yet another age-old activity—track and field. Please read on to learn more of the ministry's new guidelines for a track meet designed so that no one loses and everyone wins, because they do the best they can.

High Jump—There is no bar, as hitting it could produce an attitude of failure.

Sprint—No set distance. Participants may run in any direction they wish, as far as they wish. We feel this makes for a less stressful event.

Long Jump—In the spirit of non-competition, remember this: "It is not how far you jumped but that you jumped." The tape measure has no gradations. A jump may occur in the pit or anywhere along the runway.

Throwing Events—Participants place the shot/discus/javelin etc. in a spot that makes them feel good. The emphasis is on creativity, not brute force.

Endurance Run—Participants will run until they are tired. There is no set distance as we do not believe in encouraging students to go further than is comfortable for them.

Awards—Everyone will receive a huge trophy with everyone's name on it for each event.

In these events, we have attempted to establish a non-competitive, no failure situation. This is to prepare our young people to be successful in our non-competitive society.

Wednesday September 12

There's a little twinge of sadness
When Summer disappears,
But Autumn brings new gladness
And joys this time of year.

Elsie N. Brady

Thursday September 13

THE only thing which makes it possible to regard this world we live in without disgust is the beauty which now and then men create out of the chaos: the pictures they paint, the music they compose, the books they write and the lives they lead.

Of all these, the richest in beauty is a life well lived. That is the perfect work of art.

Somerset Maugham

Friday September 14

EXPECTING the world to treat you fairly because you are a good person is a little like expecting the bull not to attack you because you are a vegetarian.

Dennis Wholey

Saturday September 15

THIS is that time of year when sports fans are in a world of their own. The baseball season is winding down and heading into the playoffs, the football season is in full swing and the hockey season is just beginning. As Bruce remarked, "So many games ... so few hours in a day."

John told me this story about the Grey Cup football final, when it was first played on the Christian Sabbath, in 1969.

Many religious leaders objected to the game being played on a Sunday. However, one Anglican rector in Vernon, B.C. proved to be a very wise man. Canon Charles Reeve installed a colour television in the parish hall and invited the congregation to come by for a pre-game sermonette—a brief word from his Sponsor—and to stay after to enjoy the game. There was a wonderful turnout for church...and the game.

Sunday September 16

PEACE I leave with you, my peace I give unto you: not as the world giveth, give I unto you. Let not your heart be troubled, neither let it be afraid.

John 14: 27

Monday September 17

WHY, Sir, a man grows better humoured as he grows older. He improves by experience. When young he thinks himself of great consequence, and everything of importance. As he advances in life, he learns to think himself of no consequence, and little things of little importance; and so he becomes more patient and better pleased.

Samuel Johnson

Tuesday September 18

WHEREVER we are, it is but a stage on the way to somewhere else, and whatever we do, it is only a preparation to do something else that shall be different.

Wednesday September 19

Look around
and choose your own ground.

For long you'll live
and high you'll fly,
And smiles you'll give
and tears you'll cry.
And all you touch
and all you see
Is all your life
will ever be.

Author unknown

Thursday September 20

THERE is a wonderful Yiddish proverb that says, "Take life as it comes; if you want to give God a laugh, tell him your plans."

Friday September 21

TODAY we'll welcome the arrival of that most beautiful season of the year, autumn.

September is a marvellous time to enjoy the brilliant fall colours. Marg and I spent a few hours today driving in the countryside around the Kitchener-Waterloo area. The colours, although not yet at their peak, were quite lovely. We stopped at a farm that had a variety of fruits and vegetables in baskets on a table by the road. We looked about for the farmer, but found no one. It was then that Marg noticed a small cake tin with a sign saying, "All baskets $3.00. Please leave money in the tin. Make change if you need it."

Welcome Autumn!

Saturday September 22

I WONDER why it takes so little time for a child, who was afraid of the dark, to become a teenager who would like to stay out all night.

Sunday September 23

HOW excellent is thy loving kindness, O God! Therefore, the children of men put their trust under the shadow of thy wings.

Psalm 36:7

Monday September 24

When long the shadows of the wind had rolled
Green wheat was yielding to change assigned
And as by some vast magic undivined
The world was turning slowly into gold.

Edwin Arlington Robinson

Tuesday September 25

I LAUGHED when I saw this bumper sticker on the car in front of us today:

Hang up your phone and drive!

Wednesday September 26

I BELIEVE that I have included this prayer in a previous year, but as I grow older, I feel that it becomes ever more relevant.

Lord, thou knowest better than I know myself, that I am growing older and will someday be old.

Keep me from becoming talkative, and particularly from the fatal habit of thinking I must say something on every subject and every occasion.

Release me from the craving to straighten out everybody's affairs.

Keep my mind free from the recital of endless details—give me wings to get to the point.

I ask you grace enough to listen to the tales of other's pains. Help me to endure them with patience.

But seal my lips to my own aches and pains— they are increasing and my love of rehearsing them is becoming sweeter as the years go by.

Teach me the glorious lesson that occasionally it is possible that I may be mistaken.

Make me thoughtful, helpful, but not bossy. With my vast store of wisdom, it seems a pity not to use it all—but thou knowest, Lord, that I want a few friends at the end.

Thursday September 27

As I sit beside my window
Buried deep in troubled thought,
The beauty spread before me
Brings the comfort I have sought.

For up along the hilltop
Where pines are darkest green,

A single drop of colour
In a scarlet tree is seen.

Oh, who can doubt that God above
His vigilance has kept,
Who caused the very hills to glow
With colour while we slept.

A token of His handiwork
Is seen in every tree,
When nature hangs new pictures
For all the world to see.

Francis C. Caroles

Friday September 28

MOST of us set our goals early in life—the job we would like, the children we hope to have, the house we want to live in. While we need to work to attain these goals, the wisest of us will remember to appreciate everything along our path to success.

"It is good to have an end to journey toward, but it is the journey that matters in the end."

Ursula LeGuin

Saturday September 29

WE are sometimes made aware of a kindness long passed, and realize that there have been times when our friends' thoughts of us were of so pure and lofty character that they passed over us like the winds of heaven unnoticed; when they treated us not as what we were, but as what we aspired to be.

Henry David Thoreau

Sunday September 30

God, that madest earth and heaven,
Darkness and light;
Who the day for toil hast given,
For rest, the night;
May thine angel-guards defend us,
Slumber sweet thy mercy send us
Holy dreams and hopes attend us,
This livelong night.

Bishop R. Heber

October

Bright October

I know no other season
So filled with warmth and cheer
As on these bright October days
When autumntime is here.

The hills have turned from summer's green
To dazzling red and gold;
The flower beds are brighter too,
So festive to behold!

The harvest yield is gathered in;
God sends His gifts anew.
Each roadside stand, a harvest fair
That warms the heart of you!

A bluish haze on distant hills,
The maple's scarlet flame;
And oak trees dressed in Joseph-coats
Stand guard along the lane.

Of all the seasons of the year,
Each one with beauty blessed,

I hold to Autumn's warmth and cheer—
I like October best!

Kay Koffman

Tuesday October 2

TREASURE each other in the recognition that we do not know how long we will have each other.

Joshua Liebman

Wednesday October 3

I NEVER cease to be amazed by the computer and the impact that it has had on our lives. As wonderful as it is to have information so readily available, a few of us "oldsters" have noticed some unexpected problems with these incredible machines. Perhaps you feel the same way.

The computer, for the most part, is used by one individual. Many children are now spending an inordinate amount of time working and playing on the computer, to the exclusion of other activities. Although much can be learned on the computer, the lack of time spent with other children might be producing groups of young people who are socially inept and who have poor oral communication skills.

As well, it is easy for parents to be overly impressed with a very young child's ability to use new technology. A two-year-old really doesn't need to know how to use a mouse or install a CD into the CD-ROM, and, fascinating as these skills may be to parents, they should not come at the expense of far more important childhood activities such as talking, or playing with friends and family.

Thursday October 4

FOR me that solitude of the early morning is the most precious time of the day…The early morning hours symbolize for me, a rebirth; the anxieties, frustrations and woes of the previous day seem to have been washed away during the night. God has granted another day of life. He has granted another chance to do something worthwhile for humanity.

Dr. M. E. De Bakey

Friday October 5

MY brother-in-law Richard recently had cataract surgery and is now able to see much better. We can thank the skill of the opthamologist—and a number of Second World War pilots for this sight-saving surgical procedure.

In the 1940s these airmen were a medical mystery to the doctors treating their injured eyes. Bailing out of their planes when shot down during the Battle of Britain, they suffered an injury not seen before; tiny shards of the aircraft's Plexiglas canopy were embedded in their eyes.

Ordinarily the eye will reject a foreign body, working it to the surface and expelling it. However, in these cases, the eye did not react to the Plexiglas particles. It was disastrous for those young men, but led, a few years later, to the development of cataract implants.

I know Richard is grateful.

Saturday October 6

ALL across our country this weekend, families will join together for that special celebration that is a Canadian Thanksgiving. Although each family celebrates in its own way, we are all giving thanks for the harvest that is complete and for all things given to us.

You may find it interesting to know that the squash soup or pumpkin pie that you enjoy this weekend originated here in North America. Pumpkins and other members of the squash family were indigenous to the New World. The early settlers from Europe had never seen pumpkins, but when plants transported from Europe failed to thrive in the harsh Canadian climate, the settlers were very happy to discover these edible vegetables.

I plan to enjoy my pumpkin pie enormously!

Sunday October 7

Now thank we all our God,
With heart and hands and voices,
Who wondrous things has done,
In whom the world rejoices;
Who from our mother's arms
Hath blessed us on our way
With countless gifts of love,
And still is ours today.

Rev. Martin Rinkart

Monday October 8
Thanksgiving Day

AS many of our family had some distance to travel today, we enjoyed our turkey dinner yesterday. Today we are going to dine on some leftover turkey in Bruce's own special recipe for Turkey Chili. This chili can be made quite mild for people like me—or you can enjoy the hot version that is almost certain to leave a tear in your eye.

1 tbsp. canola oil
6 cups cooked turkey, diced
1 can (15 oz.) kidney beans, drained
1 can (8 oz.) tomato sauce
2 whole tomatoes, diced
1 pkg. (1 3/4 oz.) chili seasoning
2 cups water
shredded cheddar cheese
sour cream
tabasco (optional)

In a large pot, heat oil over medium heat. Add turkey; cook until golden brown, stirring continuously (about 5 minutes). Add beans, tomato sauce, tomatoes, chili seasoning and water. Mix well. Bring to a boil. Reduce heat. Cover and simmer, stirring occasionally, for 30 minutes. (If you wish, you may do this early in the day and reheat to serve.)

Serve in chili bowls, and top with a dollop of sour cream and shredded cheddar cheese. Tabasco or other hot sauce may be added for extra "zing." Serves 8.

Tuesday October 9

MY coat and I live comfortably together. It has assumed all my wrinkles, does not hurt me anywhere, has moulded itself on my deformities, and is complacent to all my movements, and I only feel its presence because it keeps me warm. Old coats and old friends are the same thing.

Victor Hugo

Wednesday October 10

ONE of the least enjoyable parts of any large family gathering is cleaning up after the meal. Marg came up with a novel approach this year, to involve every one in this rather onerous chore.

When our meal was finished, Marg brought in two baskets that contained slips of paper. One was for the adults, the other for the children, and each person was to pick one slip of paper from the correct basket.

"Clear the table" read my slip, and I was joined by Phyllis and her son Justin, whose slips of paper read the same as mine did. Each of us had an assigned chore, and with everyone laughing and helping, the cleanup was done quickly and with little grumbling. Even the little ones enjoyed their jobs—folding napkins, taking the trash out to the garage, keeping the very little ones out of trouble.

Marg's ingenuity made the cleanup an enjoyable experience for all of us, and it was over before we knew it.

Thursday October 11

Autumn
The painted hills make hearts pound.
The river runs calm and low.
Reflections of colourful trees are etched
On the water's edge below.

Shirley Hile Powell

Friday October 12

MY great-granddaughter Bethany was somewhat upset early today. A bad cold kept her home from school, and she missed her class trip to the Royal Ontario Museum.

Jamie, understanding her disappointment, found some things for them to do together. They watched a video, made cookies and spent some time just reading favourite books in bed. Although she missed being with her friends at the museum, she enjoyed the happy hours in the company of her mother. I was reminded of this line by Ralph Waldo Emerson.

For everything that you have missed you have gained something else.

Saturday October 13

THE unremembered acts of kindness are the best part of a person's life.

William Wordsworth

Sunday October 14

TRUST in the Lord with all your heart, and do not lean on your own understanding. In all your ways acknowledge Him and He will make your paths straight.

Proverbs 3:5–6

Monday October 15

MY friend Will has spent the last few weeks cleaning out his gardens and bringing inside those plants that he feels he can nurture through the winter. In our family, which is distinctly lacking in Will's expertise, we buy plants for the indoors that are classified as "plants that you can't kill." Many of the tropical foliage plants are known for their durability and seem able to survive even the most diligent of the "plant assassins" in our home.

As it was explained to me, these plants have been domesticated from the jungle and bred to be adaptable to a variety of environments.

Not only do they tolerate a range of temperatures starting as low as 40°F, they prefer indirect sunlight and sporadic watering. They are also usually pest free.

If you too are a "plant killer," here are a few of the plants that you might want to try in your home: aglaonema, schefflera, palm, deffenbachia, philodendron or spathiphyllum.

Tuesday October 16

THIS past weekend, Eleanor and I enjoyed a marvellous fall weekend in Muskoka. We were there to take part in the Bala Cranberry Festival, a tradition in this small town since 1984. The popularity of the festival has grown each year, and now crowds of 20,000 or more are common.

Cranberry growing in Ontario began in the 1940s with George Mollard. After spending many years surveying bogs and harvesting peat, he started Ontario's first commercial cranberry farm in MacTier. Orville Johnson, who as a young man worked summers on Mollard's farm, planted his own bog in Muskoka in 1952. When Mollard gave up growing cranberries, Johnston's became the only cranberry farm in Ontario. In 1969, Orville was hired to help establish a cranberry farm on the Gibson Reserve, now Whata Territory. Today, Johnston's and the Iroquois cranberry growers are still the only two commercial cranberry farms in Ontario.

This weekend, Eleanor and I enjoyed watching the berries being picked by the unique "wet rake" method at the Johnston's marsh. We drank hot cider, ate apple fritters and purchased cranberry candles and soap to take home with us. We also enjoyed seeing a multitude of crafts and antiques, and we were two very tired ladies at the end of the weekend. I can hardly wait for next year's festival.

Wednesday October 17

A DEAR friend of mine passed away this past weekend, a lovely lady whom I shall miss very much. At her funeral today, her grandson read this beautiful parable.

"I am standing upon the seashore. A ship at my side spreads her white sails in the morning breeze and starts for the blue ocean. She is an object of beauty and strength, and I can stand and watch her until, at length, she is only a ribbon of white cloud just where the sea and the sky come to mingle with each other. Then some-one at my side says 'There! She's gone!'

"Gone where? Gone from my sight—that is all. She is just as large in mast and hull and spar as she was when she left my side, and just as able to bear her load of living freight to the place of destination. Her diminished size is in me, not in her, and just at the moment when someone at my side says, 'There! She's gone!' there are other voices ready to take up the glad shout, 'There! She comes.' And that is dying."

Thursday October 18

DON'T cross your bridges until you get to them. We spend our lives defeating ourselves crossing bridges we never get to.

Bob Bales

Friday October 19

THE idea that no one is perfect is a view most commonly held by people with no grandchil-dren.

Doug Larson

Saturday October 20

FORMER U.S. vice-president Hubert H. Humphrey spoke for many of us when he said, "The good old days were never that good, believe me. The good new days are today, and better days are coming tomorrow. Our greatest songs are still unsung."

Sunday October 21

ALTHOUGH the leaves are past their peak colours now, the drive to church was still quite beautiful. How fitting that we should sing this lovely hymn, by F. S. Pierpoint.

> For the beauty of the earth,
> For the glory of the skies,
> For the love which from our birth,
> Over and around us lies,
> Lord of all to thee we raise,
> This our grateful psalm or praise.

Monday October 22

ALTHOUGH the names that we seem to remember most readily when we think of inventors are mostly those of men—Alexander Graham Bell, Henry Ford, Bill Gates—women have played a major role in developing many of the inventions that we use today. My son-in-law John was telling me today about a number of these items and the women who invented them and I admit that I knew very few of them.

Perhaps you'll find this list as interesting as I did.

Bulletproof vests—In 1965, Stephanie Kwolek invented Kevlar, the lightweight material used in bulletproof vests. It is also used in auto bodies, boats and space vehicles.

Microwave Ovens—In the 1960s, scientist Jesse Cartwight invented the Radar Range—the first microwave oven, as well as the icemaker and the delicate cycle on washing machines.

Business Computer Programming—In the 1950's, Rear Admiral Grace Murray Hopper developed the first easy-to-use computer programming language called COBOL.

Women have also invented liquid paper, cordless phones, windshield wipers, the AIDS drug AZT, solar heating, drip coffee and the indispensable disposable diapers. I guess we really are "Mothers of Invention."

Tuesday October 23

WHETHER you think you can or you think you can't, you're right.

Henry Ford

Wednesday October 24

NOBODY grows old by merely living a number of years; people grow old only by deserting their ideals. Years wrinkle the skin, but to give up enthusiasm wrinkles the soul.

You are as young as your faith, as old as your doubt; as young as your self-confidence, as old as your fear; as young as your hope, as old as your despair.

Thursday October 25

My old, oak tree has seen many a fall,
And many a winter so cold,
A new dress in spring is sparkling and green;
In October a crown of gold.
And ever she'll stand on the side of the hill
Through the wind and the rain and the snow,
Though her leaves fade and fall as November draws near
She will last through the winter, I know.
As proud and as tall as the years come and go,
She will always be standing the same,
And when it is March and the snow melts away
She will welcome the spring time again.

Garnett Ann Schultz

Friday October 26

THE only disability in my life is a bad attitude.

Scott Hamilton

Saturday October 27

JOSEPH Pulitzer offered his advice to writers, but I feel that it could easily apply to anyone who communicates with others.

"Put it before them briefly so they will read it, clearly so they will appreciate it, picturesquely so they will remember it and, above all, accurately so they will be guided by its light."

Sunday October 28

WHILE the earth remaineth, seedtime and harvest, and cold and heat, and summer and winter, and day and night shall not cease.

Genesis 8:22

Monday October 29

THE arrogance of the young is a direct result of not having known enough consequences. The turkey that every day greedily approaches the farmer who tosses him grain, is not wrong. It is just that no one ever told him about Thanksgiving.

Harry Golden

Tuesday October 30

MY friend Marcia a native of Boston, Massachusetts, usually tries to visit Salem in the month of October. In case you do not remember, Salem was the site of the witch trials in 1692, when 19 men and women were hanged, and 17 others died later in prison, after being wrongfully accused of practising witchcraft.

During October, Salem, known as "Witch City" celebrates Halloween with unbridled enthusiasm. As Marcia writes:

"In October, Salem's 'Haunted Happenings' provide activities for young and old alike, Edna.

There are haunted houses to visit, magnificent costume balls, 3-D haunted adventures, a haunted pirate ship, and spooky story times for children. There is a parade, pumpkin decorating and even gravestone rubbing. In the evening you can take a candlelit tour of the historic sites. It's well worth a yearly visit."

Wednesday October 31

On Halloween like leaves we scatter
Witches and goblins, and black cats chatter
Up a lawn, down a lane, ringing bells
Getting treats and casting spells
In Halloween moonlight what creature we'll meet
Staying up late and nibbling treats.

Author unknown

November

Thursday November 1
All Saints Day

THE dictionary defines a "saint" as a person who is exceptionally patient or charitable.

Christina Rossetti, the inspirational poet, may have been a saint in her time. Born in 1830 to a London family of modest means, Christina's life was filled with struggle. In spite of her many sorrows, she had a strong, dedicated faith and her legacy when she died, in 1894, was a collection of beautiful and inspirational poems, including the one below, entitled "Uphill."

Does the road wind up hill all the way?
Yes, to the very end.
Will the journey take the whole day?
From morn to night, my friend.

But is there for the night a resting place?
A roof for when the slow dark hours begin.
May not the darkness hide it from my face?
You cannot miss that inn.

Shall I find comfort, travel-sore and weak?
Of labour you shall find the sum.

Will there be beds for me and all who seek?
Yes beds for all who come.

Friday November 2

EACH day is an opportunity to start all over again, to cleanse our minds and hearts anew and to clarify our vision. And let us not clutter up today with the leavings of other days.

Oliver Wendell Holmes

Saturday November 3

MANY years ago my daughter Mary read an article in *Reader's Digest*. Although I don't know the story word for word, it went something like this.

A Chinese traveller was trying to make a connection between two trains. He was running late and when his bag failed to appear, he rushed to the baggage room, threw his claim check on the counter and demanded his suitcase. The attendant couldn't find it. As the minutes ticked away, the Chinese man could no longer contain himself. He pounded on the counter and shouted "Pretty damn seldom where my bag go. She no fly. You no more fit run station than godsake. That's all I hope."

To this day Mary and John use these words to end many an argument. One need only begin,

"Pretty damn seldom…" before they both end up laughing and replying in unison, "That's all I hope!"

Sunday November 4

Praise my soul, the King of Heaven;
To his feet thy tribute bring;
Ransomed, healed, restored, forgiven,
Ever more His praises sing;
Alleluia, Alleluia,
Praise the everlasting King.

Angels help us to adore him,
Ye behold him face to face;
Sun and moon bow down before him;
Dwellers all in time and space,
Alleluia, Alleluia,
Praise with us the God of grace.

Rev. H. F. Lyte

Monday November 5

November in our area is often my least favourite. After the spectacular beauty of September and October, this month seems a letdown. The trees are bare, the skies are grey, the grass is not as green. Who can find beauty and comfort in such a stark landscape? It took my son-in-law Bruce, to point out to me that with all

"After
the Harvest"

C. Black

of the leaves gone from the trees, the beautiful cardinals, blue jays and chickadees are much easier to see. He was right! Each month does provide something appealing—we just need to look for it.

Tuesday November 6

ALL persons have their frailties; and whoever looks for a friend without imperfections will never find what he seeks. We love ourselves, notwithstanding our faults, and we ought to love our friends in a like manner.

Cyrus

Wednesday November 7

OUR creator would never had made such lovely days, and have given us the deep hearts to enjoy them, above and beyond all thought, unless we were meant to be immortal.

Nathaniel Hawthorne

Thursday November 8

KNOWING, as we do now, the dangers of smoking, it is interesting to find that back in 1604, King James wrote that it was:

"A habit loathsome to the eye, hateful to the nose, harmful to the brain, dangerous to the lungs, and in the black stinking fume thereof, nearest resembling the horrible stygian smoke of the pit that is bottomless."

Friday November 9

MY sister Sarah and I talk often about our childhood on Canada's east coast. It was a quieter and gentler time and we found much to love in our small-town upbringing. I thought of these lines from Eiluned Lewis and of how much they reminded me of those days that are long gone.

We who were born in country places
Far from cities and shining faces,
We have a birthright no man can sell,
And a secret joy no man can tell.

For we are kindred to Lordly things:
The wild duck's flight and the owl's white wings,
The pike and the salmon, the bull and the
    horse,
The curlew's cry and the smell of gorse,

Pride of trees, swiftness of streams,
Magic of frost have shaped our dreams
No baser vision their spirit fills
Who walk by right on the naked hills.

Saturday November 10

IT is not enough to love those who are near and dear to us. We must show them that we do so.

Lord Avebury

Sunday November 11

TODAY we remember all those who gave their lives in the two world wars. The American, General Patton, when speaking of the casualties in his command said, "It is foolish to mourn that such men died; rather, we should thank God that such men lived."

At our service this morning we read this prayer.

Almighty God, from whom all thoughts of truth and peace proceed: Kindle, we pray thee, in the hearts of all men, the true love of peace, and guide with thy pure and peaceable wisdom those who take counsel for the nations of the earth; that in tranquility thy kingdom may go forward, till the earth is filled with the knowledge of thy love; through Jesus Christ our Lord. Amen.

Monday November 12

TALK is by far the most accessible of pleasures. It costs nothing in money, is all profit, it completes our education, founds and fosters

friendships, and can be enjoyed at any age and almost any state of health.

Robert Louis Stevenson

Tuesday November 13

BACK in 1998 when 76-year-old astronaut John Glenn was to return to space aboard the shuttle Discovery, he took a great deal of kidding about his advanced years. My friend Jake reminded me of this humourous "Top Ten" list that made us all laugh—then and now!

Top Ten changes NASA will have to make to accommodate Glenn's return to space:

10. All important devices now operated by the "Clapper."
9. Shuttle's thermostat set at 80°F.
8. Shuffle board installed in the cargo bay.
7. "Early Bird" specials from Denny's Restaurant included in the menu.
6. One monitor specifically designated to show "Matlock."
5. Little bowls of candy scattered randomly around the ship.
4. Top speed of the shuttle set for 25 mph.
3. A bifocal windshield installed.
2. Space pants now go up to the armpits.
1. Left turn blinker left on for the entire mission.

Wednesday November 14

IF faith can move mountains, imagine what hard work can do.

Thursday November 15

FOR me, there is nothing more important in my life than family. Many others share my outlook as these next thoughts will attest.

Family...the heart of so many happy memories.

A family is a place to begin and a place to belong.

Family ties so gently teach you
How to give and how to care...
And family ties so warmly reach you
Anytime and anywhere.

Anonymous

"Family" is the closeness
That our hearts will always turn to,
The warm acceptance we will always know
"Family" is the focus
That gives life its joy and meaning ...
"Family" is the love we won't outgrow.

Anonymous

Family love becomes more beautiful,
More treasured through life's changing seasons.

Marjorie Francis Ames

A family is one of nature's masterpieces.

George Santayana

Friday November 16

NOVEMBER is the month when we, in Ontario, are able to visit the Royal Agricultural Winter Fair. "The Royal," as it is known, is a unique opportunity to experience the richness of our agricultural heritage and the excellence of the agricultural and food industry that has made Canada a world leader.

Held in the Coliseum at Exhibition Place, in Toronto, The Royal is the world's largest indoor agricultural fair and international equestrian competition.

The Royal is visited annually by many hundreds of school children. For a number of them it is their first opportunity to see farm animals, and the children's enthusiasm is occasionally excessive. Let me explain:

Christy, a friend of my granddaughter Phyllis, took her grade 1 class to the fair, and all was well until she and her students entered the area where the animals were confined to the stalls. One youngster, frustrated when the lambs didn't come to the fence when he called them, found a quick solution to the problem: he climbed into the stall with them! He was so excited to be with the woolly animals that it took several minutes before Christy was able to catch his attention and convince him to exit the stall.

A visit to the Royal Agricultural Winter Fair is

truly a unique experience and one not to be missed.

Saturday November 17

MY friend Mavis Tewberry arrived today from Winnipeg, for a few days' visit. As we waited for her luggage to come down the chute she explained that she had gone to the trouble of marking her bag for easy identification.

"Yes Edna, I took a very bright pink ribbon and attached it to the handle. We shouldn't have any problem picking out my bag!"

As bag after bag came down the chute, I fixed my eyes on the handles, looking for the pink ribbon. Finally we saw it and Mavis triumphantly lifted the bag from the carousel.

I need to tell you, though, that I believe the pink ribbon was a bit superfluous. Her bag, unlike the dozens of brown, black and green ones, was a bright red, yellow and blue Harlequin-patterned duffel bag!

Sunday November 18

JUDGE not, and ye shall not be judged; condemn not, and ye shall not be condemned; forgive, and ye shall be forgiven.

Luke 6:37

Monday November 19

HOW I am enjoying Mavis' company! Although we have kept in touch through frequent letters and phone calls, it has been some time since we have seen each other. Mavis looks wonderful! She is one of those rare people who never seems to change. I believe that she will be as beautiful and full of life at 95 as she's been since I've known her. I think Oliver Wendell Holmes said it best: "To be 70 years young is sometimes far more cheerful and hopeful than to be 40 years old."

Tuesday November 20

I FIND it interesting that the meanest life, the poorest existence is attributed to God's will, but as human beings become more affluent, as their living standard and style begin to ascend the material scale, God descends the scale of responsibility at a commensurate speed.

Maya Angelou

Wednesday November 21

THINGS turn out best for the people who make the best of the way things turn out.

Art Linkletter

Thursday November 22

THIS is the day that our neighbours to the south celebrate Thanksgiving. In the United States, this holiday is the most important family occasion of the year, surpassing even Christmas in the number of travellers going home to be with loved ones. For our American friends I offer these lines:

Thanksgiving time…
a wonderful time of rich, golden harvests…
of family traditions and closeness
shared as loved ones gather near…
of beautiful memories that keep
yesterday's joys ever present in our hearts.

Friday November 23

MAVIS and I had a most extraordinary experience today. As we sat on a bench in the mall, a young person, probably about 18 or 19 years of age, sat down beside Mavis. Never one to be shy, Mavis struck up a conversation with the young lady who, it turned out, was on lunch break from the local high school. One of the girl's friends came over, and the conversation continued, including the newcomer. Soon there were half a dozen young people with Mavis and I, all of us talking as if we had known each other for years. Eventually, one of the students noticed the time, and the group bid a hasty goodbye as they left for class. They will probably never know how important they were in the day of two elderly ladies.

Saturday November 24

ONE of the nicest things about having guests from out-of-town is that we often visit "tourist" locales that we may not see from year to year. Today was one of those occasions as Bruce and Marg took Muriel and I to the Ontario Science Centre. I had nearly forgotten what a marvel the Science Centre is.

Designed by Vancouver-born architect Raymond Moriyama and built into the side of a ravine on the Don River, the centre is a series of concrete and glass structures connected by escalators. There are four main themes which incorporate hundreds of interactive displays—The Living Earth, Space Technology, The Information Highway, and the Body Science.

I particularly like the space display since I still have difficulty imagining people walking on the moon. I don't pretend to understand the workings of a space craft, but I can appreciate the brilliance of the men and women who work within the space program.

How glad I am that Mavis's visit gave us an excuse to see the Science Centre once again.

Sunday November 25

DRAW nigh to God and He will draw nigh to you...

James 4:8

Monday November 26

YOUNG people searching for their "real self" must learn that the real self is not something one finds as much as it is something one makes: and it is one's daily actions that shape the inner personality far more permanently than any amount of introspection or intellection.

Sydney J. Harris

Tuesday November 27

HUMOUR is the great thing, the saving thing. The minute it crops up, all our irritations and resentments slip away, and a sunny spirit takes their place.

Mark Twain

Wednesday November 28

DR. Harry M. Sparks, after he retired as President of Murray State University, Kentucky, found that his life was extremely busy. He explained, "I used to work for the Board of Regents, and they met every three months. Now

I work for Lois Sparks, and she meets me every morning."

Thursday November 29

IS there anything more comforting on a miserable November night than a bowl of homemade soup? This recipe for Zucchini Soup will certainly fill the bill. Served with hot biscuits and a salad, zucchini soup makes a delicious meal, perhaps to be eaten while watching tonight's hockey game.

Zucchini Soup

3 cups chopped zucchini (Peel, slice lengthwise, and scoop out seeds and pulp before chopping coarsely.)
3 cans condensed chicken broth
1 cup water
4 tbsp. butter
1 chopped onion
1 tbsp. parsley flakes
2 or 3 celery leaves, chopped
pinch of thyme
salt & pepper to taste
1 cup cream

Put vegetables in a pot with broth and water. In a skillet over heat, sauté the onion in butter for 5 minutes until soft. Add onions and butter to the soup pot along with parsley, celery leaves, thyme, salt and pepper. Cover and simmer for 20 minutes. Purée the soup in a blender until smooth. Add cream, reheat and serve. Serves 6.

Friday November 30

MY friend Emily, who winters in Florida, amused me with this story.

"Every year before Christmas, Edna, our condominium organization holds an 'Elegante Junque Sale.' Really it's just another name for a garage sale, but often many of the items contributed for the sale are new or little used, because the money collected is used to buy Christmas toys for less fortunate families.

"On the morning of the sale, my good friends Betty and Jim wanted to look at different items, so they agreed to meet back at the cashier's desk in 45 minutes.

"Betty found several items to buy, and Jim was extremely enthusiastic over the 'treasures' that he found. When they got home, Betty couldn't help but laugh. Four of the articles that Jim had bought were things that Betty had donated to the sale!

"Oh well! It's all for a good cause."

December

Saturday December 1

WE awoke this morning to find the ground covered with a layer of snow. As I looked out my window at the beauty of this white carpet, I was reminded of the poem "First Snow." Thanks to the unknown author for these lovely lines.

Sometime last night snow began to fall
So gently did it come, so softly white;
It's music we failed to hear at all
As it whispered its song to the listening night.

The star snowflakes still swirl about,
Veiling the barn and the pasture lot;
Veiling the view when I look out
Of the distant lake and maple plot.

The evergreens with snow are spread,
Drifts push up against the wall.
Each post wears a nightcap on its head,
Everything's dressed in the new snowfall.

It is good to be in this world of white,
Silent but for the murmur of the snow,

And the sighing of my wood fire bright
That makes my kitchen all aglow.

It is pure and beautiful outside—
Within my room is cosy and warm.
A sense of peace with me abides
As I look out at the first snowstorm.

Sunday December 2

ALMIGHTY God, give us grace that we may
cast away the works of darkness, and put
upon us the armour of light, now in the time of
this mortal life, in which thy Son Jesus Christ
came to visit us in great humility; that in the last
day, when he shall come again in his glorious
Majesty to judge both the quick and the dead, we
may rise to the life immortal, through him who
liveth and reigneth with thee and the Holy Spirit,
now and ever. Amen

Collect for the first Sunday in Advent

Monday December 3

AS we move ever closer to Christmas, and the
hustle and bustle of the season threatens to
wear us down, it is important to remember why
we are celebrating.

Take time to think about the child born in that humble stable so very long ago. Take time to rejoice in his birth. Don't lose sight of what Christmas means. At times it is difficult to see through the trappings of the holiday and to remember why we celebrate.

Take time.

Tuesday December 4

AT this time of year, when almost all social occasions offer delicious and tempting treats to eat, many people find it easy to put on a few extra pounds. My son-in-law Bruce who regularly fights the "battle of the bulge" made us all laugh with these "Rules for Dieting:"

If you eat something and no one sees you eat it, it has no calories.

If you drink a diet pop with a chocolate bar, the calories in the chocolate bar are cancelled out by the diet pop.

When you eat with someone else, calories don't count if you don't eat more than they do.

Foods used for medicinal purposes never count, such as hot chocolate, brandy, toast, and Sara Lee cheesecake.

Cookie pieces contain no calories. The process of breaking causes calorie leakage.

Foods that have the same colour have the

same number of calories, for example, spinach and pistachio ice cream, pink grapefruit and ham, beets and steak.

Chocolate is a universal colour and may be substituted for any other food colour.

Anything consumed while standing has no calories. This is due to gravity and the density of the caloric mass.

Anything consumed from someone else's plate has no calories since the calories rightfully belong to the other person and will cling to his or her plate.

Wednesday December 5

WE have only this minute, sparkling like a star in our hand and melting like a snowflake. Let us use it before it's too late.

M. E. Beynon

Thursday December 6

IT'S thought that more than two and a half billion greeting cards will be sent throughout North America this holiday season. When Bruce saw the stack of cards that Marg and I were working on, he laughingly remarked, "Those billions were for all of North America—not just this household."

The sending and receiving of Christmas cards

is one of my favourite traditions of the season. I am always thrilled to hear from old friends and acquaintances from many parts of the world, and I hope that they look forward to my cards as much as I look forward theirs. Marg and I like to include a personal note with each card, so writing them is a time consuming job. I like to think of it as a labour of love.

Friday December 7

THE best thing about growing older is that it takes such a long time.

Walters Kemp

Saturday December 8

With all that there is to do at this time of year, the holiday season may be stressful for many people. Over dinner this evening, several of my "senior" friends and I discussed some ways to lesson the strain of "too much to do—too little time."

Here are just a few of our ideas—perhaps you have others.

This first suggestion may sound simple, but I believe it is a good one. Do one thing at a time. Often we will start one project, think of another and then do a good job with neither. Start and finish just one thing and then move on.

Muriel likes to get up 15 minutes earlier each morning. "Those few extra minutes allow me to get myself organized before I start on the jobs that need doing."

Don't rely on your memory. Write down, on a list, those things that you want to accomplish each day. There is an old Chinese proverb that says, "The palest ink is better than the most retentive memory."

When shopping, be prepared to wait. A paperback to read can make a wait in a post office line almost pleasant.

Unplug your phone for an hour when you want to work uninterrupted.

Make some time for yourself each day—you'll enjoy the season so much more.

Sunday December 9

BLESSED Lord, who hast caused all holy scriptures to be written for our learning; Grant that we may in such wise hear them, read, mark, learn. And inwardly digest them, that by patience, and comfort of thy holy Word, we may embrace, and ever hold fast the blessed hope of everlasting life, which thou hast given us in our Saviour Jesus Christ. Amen

Collect for the Second Sunday in Advent

Monday December 10

Christmas is star-shine in every man's sky,
Laughter and wonder in every child's eye:
Shepherds and angels caroling clear,
Heaven brought down for a moment each
year.

A. M. Swaim

Tuesday December 11

I DON'T know what your destiny will be, but one thing I know: the only ones among you will be truly happy are those who have sought and found how to serve.

Albert Schweitzer

Wednesday December 12

I DO enjoy the music of the Christmas season. One of the loveliest carols is also one of the most often sung, "O Holy Night."

O Holy night! The stars are brightly shining
It is the night of our dear Saviour's birth.
Long lay the world, in sin and error pining
'Til He appeared and the soul felt His worth.
A thrill of hope, the weary world rejoices,
For yonder breaks a new and glorious morn!
Fall on your knees!
O hear the angel voices!

O night divine! O night when Christ was born!
O night divine! O night, O night divine!

Thursday December 13

THIS is the time of year when many of us have unexpected guests stop in to bring personal wishes for the season. Marg and Bruce like to have plenty of finger food snacks to serve and Rumaki—chicken livers wrapped in bacon— really add a special touch to any hors d' oeuvres tray.

Rumaki

12 chicken livers, halved at the natural separation
24 thin slivers of water chestnut
12 slices of bacon, halved
1 1/2 cups soy sauce
1 clove minced garlic
1 cup light brown sugar

Make a small incision in the centre of each chicken liver half, and insert a sliver of water chestnut. Wrap each piece of liver in a piece of bacon, and hold in place with a toothpick.

Mix soy sauce and garlic, and add chicken livers. Cover and marinate in the refrigerator for several hours (or 30 minutes if really pressed for time).

Just before serving, remove livers from the marinade, roll lightly in brown sugar and broil until the bacon is crisp. Serve hot.

Friday December 14

GOD gave us memory so that we might have roses in December.

James M. Barrie

Saturday December 15

ONE of the loveliest Christmas decorations is the poinsettia. This plant's tiny flowers, surrounded by large flower-like leaves turn a brilliant red (or less commonly, pink, or white) in the winter months. The poinsettia is native to Mexico and was first brought to America in 1828 by Joel Roberts Poinsett, a botanist and the first American ambassador to Mexico.

There is a lovely Mexican legend that comes with the poinsettia plant. Pablo, a poor young Mexican boy, wanted to bring a gift to Jesus at the shrine of the nativity. Too poor to buy a gift, Pablo broke off a branch of the plant. When he placed the plant at the altar, it is said that the leaves miraculously turned a brilliant red, and his gift was transformed into a beautiful flower.

Today, the poinsettia plant rivals holly as one of the most popular plants for Christmas.

Sunday December 16

> O come, O come, Emmanuel,
> And ransom captive Israel,
> That morns in lowly exile here,
> Until the Son of God appear.
> Rejoice! Rejoice! Emmanuel
> Shall come to thee, O Israel.

Translated from Latin by Rev. J. M. Neale

Monday December 17

NINETY-EIGHT years ago, Orville and Wilbur Wright made their historic first flight in an airplane. How incredible that in less than 100 years humankind has gone from a rather shaky 12-second flight to walking on the moon, and now is looking at the possibility of living for long periods of time in space stations. Who can guess where future generations may fly?

Tuesday December 18

> Live not in yesterdays,
> Look back and you may sorrow.
> Live precisely for today,
> Look forward to tomorrow.

Author unknown

Wednesday December 19

HANUKKAH, the Jewish celebration of religious freedom, takes place about the time of the winter solstice, and lasts for eight days. A special time for children, it is a time for song and games and gift-giving in Jewish homes.

May I wish, for all of my Jewish friends, the joy of the season and a very happy Hanukkah!

Thursday December 20

The Christmas tree with its candles gleamimg,
A glow is kindling in our hearts,
It speaks of God's pure love-light streaming,
It brings us hope and joy imparts.

Friday December 21

This is the day of the winter solstice, the first day of our long winter season.

Tis winter, yet there is no sound along the air
Of winds along their battle-ground; but gently
    there
The snow is falling all around.

Ralph Hunt

Saturday December 22

AT this time of year, many people wonder what to buy for elderly relatives. Here are a few of my favourite suggestions:

A prepaid phone card. Many of us would like to keep in touch with far-off friends, and long distance calling is expensive.

Restaurant gift certificates. For those of us on a fixed budget, eating out is an almost impossible luxury.

Books on tapes. As our old eyes get weaker, it is wonderful to enjoy the printed word with our ears.

Your time. Nothing is a finer gift than time spent in your presence.

Sunday December 23

Fourth Sunday in Advent

See amid the winter's snow,
Born for us on earth below;
See the tender lamb appears,
Promised from eternal years.
Hail thou ever blessed morn;
Hail, redemption's happy dawn;
Sing through all Jerusalem,
Christ is born in Bethlehem.

Rev. E. Caswall

Monday December 24

MARG, Bruce and I worked very hard this weekend, and we're now completely ready for the big day. With today free of last minute-activities, we decided to spend our time at the local nursing home, helping out wherever we could. We found many ways to be of assistance. Bruce enjoyed hanging Christmas cards on the walls for all to see, while Marg and I wrapped gifts that had been donated to the residents by local merchants. At noon we were all involved in feeding those residents who were unable to feed themselves. The Christmas music that played during lunch time brought a smile to every face.

"The only gift is a portion of yourself."

Ralph Waldo Emerson

Tuesday December 25

Christmas Day

AND the angel said unto them, Fear not: for, behold, I bring you good tidings of great joy, which shall be to all people.

For unto you is born this day in the city of David a Saviour, which is Christ the Lord.

And this shall be a sign unto you; Ye shall find the babe wrapped in swaddling clothes, lying in a manger.

And suddenly there was with the angel a multitude of the heavenly host praising God, and saying,

Glory be to God in the highest, and on earth peace, good will toward men.

Luke 2:10–14

Wednesday December 26

BOXING Day, which we celebrate here in Canada, is a part of our British heritage. The name came from the tradition of sending Christmas boxes of food and money to errand boys, porters, postmen and others, to show appreciation for their jobs well done during the year.

Today, the term "Boxing Day" would seem to apply to all of the items that are boxed and sold at the giant sales held at most stores! For me, it is a delightful day to rest after the excitement of yesterday.

Thursday December 27

ONE of the Christmas gifts that I prize most this year came from my great-granddaughter Bethany. Knowing how much I love flowers, Beth collected a wide variety of summer flowers and carefully pressed them in waxed paper under a number of heavy books. Later, when the flowers were pressed and dried, she glued them to a piece of paper on which she had drawn and coloured a lovely vase. Jamie and Marshall then took her to the art shop, where she chose an exquisite frame in which to place her work. The result is a wonderful piece of art that now graces my bedroom wall. I shall treasure the work of this thoughtful child forever.

Friday December 28

WHAT is it to stay young? It is the ability to hold fast to old friends, and to make new ones, to keep forever our beloved in dear remembrance, and to open our hearts quickly to a light knock on the door.

Cornelia Rogers

Saturday December 29

GOD'S best gift to us is not the things, but opportunities.

Sunday December 30

O GOD, who makest us glad with the yearly remembrance of the birth of thy only Son, Jesus Christ. Grant that as we joyfully receive him as our Redeemer, we may, with sure confidence, behold him when he shall come to be our Judge; who liveth and reigneth with thee and the Holy Spirit, now and ever. Amen.

Monday December 31

AS we come to the end of the year, it is a wonderful opportunity to look back at the year just past and forward to the year to come.

We cannot change that which is past, but we can resolve to use each day in the coming year to enjoy our lives to the fullest.

"Look not mournfully into the past. It comes not back again. Wisely improve the Present. It is thine. Go forth to meet the shadowy Future, without fear, and with a manly heart."

Henry Wadsworth Longfellow

May I wish to one and all a Happy New Year!